THE

PRIVACY

INSIDER

THE PRIVACY INSIDER

How to Embrace Data Privacy and Join the Next Wave of Trusted Brands

ARLO GILBERT

FOUNDING CEO, osano

Osano Books

Osano Books

Osano, Inc., a Public Benefit Corp

3800 N Lamar Blvd.

Austin, Texas 78756

Hardcover ISBN: 979-8-9902982-1-7 | Paperback ISBN: 979-8-9902982-0-0

Ebook ISBN: 979-8-9902982-2-4 | Audiobook ISBN: 979-8-9902982-3-1

Cover design and book design by Zoe Norvell

Nothing in this book, nor any portion thereof constitutes
actual legal or regulatory advice, opinion, or recommendation.
If legal assistance is required, please seek the services of an attorney.

This book is a tribute to the remarkable people who make Osano the leading data privacy platform in the world. You are not only my colleagues, but my friends and mentors. You have enriched my knowledge and understanding of the significance of simplicity, transparency, and empowerment in data privacy. I admire your passion, creativity, and dedication to our mission and vision.

I also want to express my gratitude to our thousands of customers and partners, who have trusted us to help them navigate the complex and evolving landscape of data privacy compliance and management. You are the driving force behind our innovation and growth. I appreciate your support, feedback, and collaboration, and I hope this book will offer you valuable insights and guidance.

Most of all, I want to thank my family, who are my everything. To my children, Daylyn, Sari, Reid, and Goldie, you are the light of my life and the reason I breathe. You make me proud and hopeful for the future. I love you more than you can know. And to my brilliant and patient wife, Alex, you are my rock, my soulmate, and my best friend. Thank you for supporting me with your encouragement, wisdom, and love.

CONTENTS

Introduction: Be the Tom Hanks of Privacy Practices   1

PART 1: How We Got Here

Chapter 1: It Started Long before the Internet   13

Chapter 2: How Our Data Gets into So Many Hands   25

Chapter 3: Why We Should Care about What the
    Government Knows about Us   49

Chapter 4: What Is Personal Information, Anyway?   67

Chapter 5: Data-Privacy Laws, and What They Mean for You   91

PART 2: Building Your Privacy Program

Chapter 6: A Bird's-Eye View of Your Privacy Program   123

Chapter 7: Governance & Accountability   141

Chapter 8: Compliance, Audit & Review   165

Chapter 9: Notice, Consent & Choice   189

Chapter 10: Risk, Response & Resilience   221

Conclusion: Compliance Is Just the Beginning   239

About the Author   241

About Osano   243

Additional Resources   245

Notes   247

Be the Tom Hanks of Privacy Practices

Yes, You Can Be the Good Guy *and* Highly Successful

Facebook had been paying off settlements for careless data handling for years when it was revealed in 2015 that they may have improperly shared up to eighty-seven million people's profile information with the political consulting firm Cambridge Analytica.[1] The *New York Times* reported that Cambridge Analytica created psychographic profiles of people based on that data to help the Trump campaign influence voter behavior in the 2016 US presidential election.[2] That scandal marked a tipping point for public awareness about data privacy, as it showed us how our personal data can be used in ways we're completely unaware of.

Perhaps it's not a shock that tech giants like Facebook mishandle our personal data. After all, we've seen the headlines about data breaches that expose consumers' information. It's become almost routine to hear about companies paying out millions in settlements over privacy violations. Beyond the headlines, our own online activity often signals to us that our personal data gets around. Targeted ads are sometimes *so* spot-on that we suspect advertisers may know more about us than they should.

The truth is that companies of all sizes have been collecting and sharing our personal data—often unethically—since the dawn of the internet. Why? Because they can. Regulators and legislators are now working hard to make sure this happens in a way that prioritizes individuals' right to privacy.

A few bad players have thrown both businesses and individuals into a trust crisis. Internet users don't know who they can trust with their data. And businesses now need to build trust with their users and customers in ways they never had to think about before.

Addressing Our Global Trust Crisis

There is a growing (and often justified) distrust in technology companies. Regulations now exist to give individuals control over how their personal data is used. We all need protection, whether we realize it or not, because the problems linked to poor data handling run deeper than leaked credit card numbers or creepy targeted ads. When our personal information gets into the wrong hands, it can be used to manipulate us, create community discord, and even persecute us. Globally, we've experienced a massive loss of trust that companies and organizations will handle our private data appropriately.

Data-privacy regulations are great news for individuals. But the responsibility for businesses to comply can feel like a tremendous burden—especially for organizations that haven't been intentional about how they store, handle, and process their users' data. As new regulations go into effect, it can seem like they put companies at risk of noncompliance nearly overnight, with consequences including financial penalties, reputational damage, and bans on operations.

This dilemma is at the heart of our work at Osano. In 2018, alongside my friend and longtime business partner Scott Hertel, I founded Osano to create tools that empower generalists to easily build and operationalize their organization's privacy programs. We're a certified B Corporation with a mission to bring simplicity to data privacy and be a force for positive change through greater data-processing transparency. We believe that data privacy is a fundamental human right and the companies that embrace privacy will become the next wave of trusted brands. We've created the tools to help companies comply with regulations and bring trust back into the equation so their consumers feel confident their data is handled ethically.

If you see data-privacy regulations as a compliance headache, this book will shift your mindset to appreciate that it's also a huge opportunity to set yourself apart from your competition as a brand consumers can trust. You can be the Tom Hanks of data privacy—credible, solid, consistent, and also massively successful.

Handling data responsibly is not just legally required. It directly impacts your bottom line. Data practices influence brand trust more than ever, as companies are losing customers daily due to poor data handling. Research from IBM shows that 75 percent of consumers will not buy from a business, no matter how great the products are, if they don't trust the company to protect their data.[3] Every time we ask folks to accept a cookie policy, agree to a privacy protocol, buy our product, or share any information online, it's a chance to stand out as a trustworthy brand. Search engine DuckDuckGo has shown us what's possible when a company makes privacy a top priority. They're an internet browser that doesn't track your search history.

In a world where mega search engines like Google and Yahoo have ruled for decades and relied on tracking user activity for revenue, DuckDuckGo exceeded $100 million in annual revenue by 2021, despite Google's near monopoly on search.[4] In the email world, Proton Mail has had similar success. They're a private email service that uses end-to-end encryption to secure email messages so that no one, not even Proton, can read them. In 2023, nine years after launching thanks to a public crowdfunding campaign, Proton had one hundred million users.[5]

Some tech giants also show us it's possible to thrive while prioritizing data. Apple's been known to take data privacy seriously. How does this look in practice? Well, consider location data. Governments can issue search warrants that require tech companies to share personal data they have about their users. Google has historically collected and stored their users' location data. Law enforcement agencies know this, and therefore, Google received more than twenty thousand of these warrants between 2018 and 2020.[6] Apple does not collect and store location data about their users. That's likely why Apple only received thirteen such search warrants in 2022. And even when those came in, Apple didn't have the data to share.[7] Folks love Apple because of their products, but it takes more than sleek phones and laptops to thrive. The trust they've earned through their data practices has made a huge contribution to their brand's longevity.

People are paying attention. Audiences expect more than the status quo. Prioritizing data privacy isn't a marketing fad. It's become a basic part of corporate compliance, and above all, it's just the right thing to do. The world's most trusted brands will be those companies that can adapt and put reputable privacy practices at the core of their operations.

This means big changes to business as usual for many companies. Some firms have spent decades collecting as much data as possible with the hope that they can monetize it someday. In the process, they've accumulated stashes of personal information that put them at risk for noncompliance under new regulations. Often, they don't even know what data they have or where it's stored. This is more common than you might think. When we started Osano in 2018, firms scrambled to understand and comply with the European Union's General Data Protection Regulation (GDPR)—and that was just the beginning. Since then, the GDPR has stirred the public's consciousness around data privacy, and major regulations have cropped up around the world, from Brazil's General Law for the Protection of Personal Data (LGPD) and the California Privacy Rights Act (CPRA) to more than a dozen state-specific laws throughout the United States. Data-privacy compliance has come to feel like a major curveball for companies as they try to navigate the growing list of laws with which they need to comply.

How to Earn Trust, Stay Compliant, and Ethically Leverage Data

. . . all without losing your mind. I promise it's possible, and this book will teach you how. Compliance will be a top priority as you create your privacy program, but a big reason I wrote this book is to highlight how important it is to look beyond regulations and think about what's right when collecting and processing consumers' personal data. It helps to see the big picture by simplifying best data practices into basic principles that I've dubbed the "kindergarten rules" for data privacy. They are:

Don't take something without asking permission. Whether you call it permission, consent, or opting in, you must ask consumers before you collect their data and specify what kind of information you want and why.

Be honest about where you're keeping someone's things. You gain consumers' trust with transparency about where their data is stored, how that data is kept private, and which third parties, if any, you share this information with.

If someone wants something of theirs that you have, give it back. You don't own consumer data; you only borrow it. If anyone asks you to remove some or all of their data, the right thing is to immediately give back what does not belong to you.

Of course, there's more to data privacy than these principles. But complex regulations do ultimately boil down to these basic ideas, which are rooted in human morals. I've been an entrepreneur throughout the entire evolution of the internet and have seen the pendulum swing from a completely unregulated Wild West landscape to an exceedingly complicated and confusing jumble of rules and laws that seem impossible to understand, much less implement. I cofounded Osano to simplify compliance and help people navigate the confusion.

In the early days of the internet, the concept that data belonged to anyone did not exist. As a result, it was commonplace to trade lists, email credit card numbers, and track people without telling them. The general consensus was that if someone voluntarily visited your website, your digital property, you were under no obligation to follow any rules. People forget (and perhaps some never grasped) that we all get to enjoy free content online because we give up our personal data in exchange for that content. That's the trade-off we agree to when we use a website. The way that ecosystem works is incredibly difficult to understand, so for a long time, most internet users didn't realize all the ways in which companies were using their data—or how those actions could violate an individual's right to privacy. Many still don't know.

Society didn't begin to grasp how extensively companies were using our data until a handful of big players were caught mismanaging it. By that time, businesses had been monetizing our data for decades. And there's nothing wrong with this when it's done responsibly and ethically. The problem was that there were no regulations to set limits on what businesses could do with personal data. And, absent regulations, they did what many successful companies do: they pushed boundaries and found innovative ways to make money. For a long time, nobody questioned those practices—even if they weren't ethical—since there were no regulations in place that demanded anything different. But times have changed. Now, simply being in business requires companies to comply with data-privacy regulations if they want to *stay* in business.

The historic lack of data regulations doesn't excuse irresponsible data handling. Companies need to be held accountable for unethical data practices. But the reality is that the internet wouldn't have evolved into the incredible resource that it is today if companies couldn't monetize our data. So much good has come out of the exchange of data for free online content. We have access to massive catalogs of research, educational resources, entertainment, and free services that benefit us every day. I don't want that to go away. I don't see data brokers or businesses that collect, store, and sell data as bad. They're important players in the evolution toward a more transparent internet. My goal for this book is to share the knowledge and skills I learned in the process of building Osano and exploring the world of data privacy. The new frontier is keeping the internet free and open while making it safer for everyone, even our kids. I care about my family's ability to confidently shop online, communicate with friends, and learn new things without the constant feeling of being stalked, watched, and profiled.

This isn't the end of data as a good thing. One of the biggest concerns companies share with us is the fear that they won't be able to analyze data for business intelligence, monetize it, or sell it to advertisers and data brokers. That's not the case. It's just that *how* you collect, store, and use it is now being regulated more than ever, and getting these tasks right can be one of the most important factors in your company's success and longevity.

How we handle data has changed, but you can still leverage it in ways that are profitable *and* privacy-law compliant. I built Osano from both perspectives, business and personal. I combine three decades of building successful businesses with being a consumer myself, plus parenting four kids who don't know a world without the internet. Working with more than forty-thousand Osano clients, I've learned that once companies adopt strong privacy programs, they not only reduce risk, but often find they *achieve more* with *less* data. They're no longer just exchanging data for revenue. They're bolstering their brand and profits in ways that other companies completely miss. Gaining that advantage requires shifting your mindset, adapting your processes, and staying informed on the ever-evolving data-privacy landscape. You are holding the playbook that will show you how to make that happen.

Your Blueprint for Profits with Principles

In this book, you'll find decades' worth of Osano's combined team experience with data privacy. The regulations are and will remain complicated, but excellent data hygiene doesn't have to be. This book breaks down the key actions you can take immediately to manage personal data ethically and illuminates where you need to focus your time and resources. We'll cover:

- How privacy requirements will impact your business.
- The regulations you need to comply with today and guidance for staying up to date on new and evolving regulations.
- How to audit and update your current data-handling practices.

- How to create a privacy program that inspires trust, keeps you compliant, and gives you a competitive advantage.

We'll start with a brief and surprising history of why data privacy is so important. (Spoiler alert: it started long before the internet.) I promise that blast from the past won't be boring but instead will clarify why we should care deeply about what businesses and governments know about us and where to draw the line running our own companies. This book will help you succeed in this newly regulated era by laying out a clear path forward and empowering you with the right information instead of overwhelming you with irrelevant details. The chapters ahead will help you navigate the privacy ecosystem and arm you with the strategy you need to become a long-lasting, successful, trusted brand.

PART 1

HOW WE GOT HERE

CHAPTER 1

It Started Long before the Internet

I t's easy to mistake data-privacy regulations for just another compliance nuisance. Yes, they are red tape that your company hadn't needed to worry about only a few years ago. But most people don't realize that data-privacy laws have their roots in protecting human rights or that they came about *because* so many individuals' rights were exploited through the systemic misuse of personal data. That may be hard to imagine when most conversations around compliance relate to cookie consent banners and privacy policies. In many ways, we're lucky we've come so far that we, as consumers, can now exercise our privacy rights with the tap of a finger. That progress stands on the shoulders of generations of effort to get legislators to acknowledge individuals' right to privacy. And the struggle isn't over. Personal data is still accessed by others in questionable ways and used to target data subjects— whether it's to advertise to them, harass them, or otherwise exploit them.

This book starts with a quick history lesson because it's so important to realize that data privacy is about more than checking a compliance box. It's about protecting our fundamental right to privacy and the rights of our fellow humans. When you know the story behind the bureaucracy, it helps to see your privacy program for what it really is: a framework for building trust with anyone who interacts with your company.

So How Did We Get Here?

If we want to see data privacy as more than just a complex headache, like our taxes, it helps to know how we got here. It started long before computers. The earliest privacy regulations date back to seventeenth century English common law and the Castle Doctrine, which established the legal theory that a person's home is their castle, and their castle is their safest refuge.[8] The law gave individuals the right to defend themselves and their homes against intruders, even if it meant killing an attacker in self-defense.

That may sound extreme compared to, say, protecting someone's email messages or debit card information, but the Castle Doctrine played a fundamental role in society's evolving perspectives on privacy. It was one of the first laws to grant people the right to a safe, personal space. Four hundred years later, what we consider "personal space" extends way beyond our home. And while we can't kill someone to defend everything that we consider private, the spirit of the law still resonates. We all want the right to protect what's personal to us.

US colonists brought English common law across the pond with them, and societal perspectives on privacy kept evolving with cultural, political, and technological advancements. The Quartering Act, passed in 1765, put a huge strain on citizens' right to feel safe in their homes. The law required colonists to house British soldiers. People's private residences were spared, but colonists were forced to furnish lodging for British soldiers wherever they could: in their inns, stables, barns, alehouses, unoccupied buildings—even their outhouses.[9] The enemy was, by law, living among them. This was bad on multiple levels. In practice, colonists resented having the opposition outside their door. British soldiers lived close enough to eavesdrop on them, which was not only a nuisance and a violation of privacy but actually a criminal offense under English common law.[10] But perhaps even worse, the situation was government mandated. In the pages ahead we'll explore why a government's infringement on its people's privacy can be more dangerous than we may realize.

The Quartering Act sparked so much civil unrest among colonists that it influenced the Declaration of Independence, which counted among its grievances against King George III the "Quartering [of] large bodies of armed troops among us."[11] The Constitution's Third Amendment defies the Quartering Act, stating that, "No Soldier shall, in time of peace be quartered in any house, without the consent of the Owner, nor in time of war, but in a manner to be prescribed by law."[12] Colonists stood firm: they wanted the government to stay out of their private lives.

While the phrase "right to privacy" doesn't appear in the Constitution, the implications are certainly there. The Fourth Amendment defends "the right of the people to be secure in their persons, houses, papers, and effects, against unreasonable searches and seizures," and the Fifth says, among other things, that "private property [shall not] be taken for public use, without just compensation." The Castle Doctrine was at least a century-old concept by the time the Constitution was written, but it was as relevant as ever. Colonists were doubling down on their right to a private, secure home, and they wanted just as much privacy for their personal affairs.

The United States' Slow Crawl to Privacy Rights

It would take another one hundred years for the phrase "right to privacy" to enter the American lexicon. We can thank an 1890 article by lawyers Louis Brandeis and Samuel D. Warren for finally articulating the concept. When the article was published, society had hit a new breaking point in its perspectives on privacy. This time it wasn't war or politics that sparked the uproar—it was the media.

The printing press was one of the first technologies to influence people's opinions on privacy. Before newspapers became popular, gossip was a serious threat that could ruin reputations and economic prospects. But newspapers took the dangers of word of mouth to new heights. Now, gossip had more longevity and could cause more damage if it appeared in print. It didn't help that the newspaper industry's biggest pioneers, William Randolph Hearst and Joseph Pulitzer, were in fierce competition at the time, and they relied on drama to lure readers to their papers.[13] Yet having one's personal business in print wasn't the only problem; newspapers were also publishing photos without the subjects' consent.

Folks felt so violated by the possibility of their private business appearing in print that the outcry incited Brandeis and Warren's article in the December 15, 1890, issue of *The Harvard Law Review*. The article, called "The Right to Privacy," was a call to action, arguing that while an individual's right to privacy may be implied in common law, it should receive the explicit protection of the criminal law.[14]

Brandeis and Warren's concerns are timeless, despite the article having been published more than 130 years ago. Technology and media platforms may have changed since 1890, but much like the Castle Doctrine, the human need for privacy holds strong today. Among their concerns, they noted that "instantaneous photographs and newspaper enterprise have invaded the sacred precincts of private and domestic life; and numerous mechanical devices threaten to make good the prediction that 'what is whispered in the closet shall be proclaimed from the house-tops.'" They're talking about nineteenth century newspapers exposing people's private affairs in print, but they could just as easily have been talking about Pamela Anderson and Tommy Lee's sex tape leaking to the public in 1996 or any paparazzi photographer who turns a profit by selling photos of people going about their daily lives.

The authors warned, "The press is overstepping in every direction the obvious bounds of propriety and of decency. Gossip is no longer the resource of the idle and of the vicious, but has become a trade." Truly, not much has changed over several centuries. It's remarkable how accurately their words describe the way most money is earned through the internet: your personal information is collected in exchange for access to content. In other words, the internet has opened up a trade that exists because companies can make money off of your data. We hope that companies won't overstep the bounds of decency when they process our private information, but that's just the problem. We'll see in the chapters ahead that our private information is sometimes exploited in alarming and surprising ways.

It turns out that advancements in technology only confirmed Brandeis and Warren's fears that instant photos would put people's "right to be let alone," as they described it, at great risk. They'd pointed out that before portable cameras, subjects had to sit to have their photo taken. This required their consent and gave them some control over how they were photographed. That all changed as camera technology evolved. A decade after the *Harvard Law Review* article was published, portable cameras became more accessible than ever with the release of Kodak's Brownie camera in 1900 for just one dollar (roughly thirty-five dollars in today's US currency). Suddenly, anyone could be a photographer. And the timing couldn't have been worse for those who valued their privacy.

The Brownie camera hit the market when Hearst and Pulitzer's newspaper wars, which feasted on gossip-laden content, were in full swing. It was a troubling combination: newspapers were eager for salacious news, and now anyone could easily take candid photos of others without their consent. The Brownie camera's popularity fueled what came to be known as yellow journalism—a style of journalism that relied on sensationalized and scandalous news to draw attention. Nobody's privacy was safe as gossip could now spread and ruin reputations at new speeds.

As technology, the media, and cultural perspectives on privacy evolved into the twentieth century, Brandeis and Warren's article had a substantial influence on the privacy landscape. It filled the gaps as an authoritative source on good privacy practices at a time when related laws were lacking. Tort scholar William Prosser found that by 1960, Brandeis and Warren's article had inspired more than three hundred privacy-related cases.[15] The Supreme Court finally recognized the "right to privacy" in *Griswold v. Connecticut* (1965), stating that specific guarantees in the Bill of Rights create "zones of privacy" formed within the shadows of what is promised, even if a "right to privacy" isn't explicitly stated.[16] The right to privacy was also the basis for several Supreme Court decisions, including women's abortion rights recognized through *Roe v. Wade* in 1973 and same-sex marriage rights recognized through *Obergefell v. Hodges* in 2015.

Brandeis and Warren would be happy to see how far data-privacy regulations have come today—but they'd also likely feel that we have a long way to go. As of this writing, the United States still doesn't have a federal data-privacy regulation, despite the promise of certain proposed laws like the American Data Privacy and Protection Act (ADPPA).

I understand that the thought of *more* regulations in the pipeline may sound intimidating. It's hard enough to comply with those regulations already on your list, and for many readers, that list is getting longer every day. Companies need to comply with data-privacy regulations based upon their users' country and state of citizenship. This means that if you hope to engage a geographically diverse audience, you must comply with regulations that are in place worldwide. The biggest in terms of global reach is the European Union's GDPR. Several others exist on national, state, and industry levels, but many of those are based on, or at least informed by, the GDPR.

The GDPR is comprehensive, strict, long, dense, and, frankly, overwhelming. The EU has historically been very protective of data privacy, and the GDPR is their most thorough regulation to date. It's easy to see it as a nuisance and simply plod through the tasks required to stay compliant, but it's worth understanding the history behind the EU's extreme caution. Its origins stem from World War II. Most people wouldn't imagine that data-privacy laws as we know them today would be linked to a war that predates the internet by decades. But once we understand the role that personal data played in violating millions of people's human rights, the connection (and the EU's concern) becomes very clear.

Why the EU Is a Leader in Data Privacy

Germany gave us the world's first data-protection law when the Hessian Data Protection Act went into effect in 1970.[17] While it was small in the sense that it was only on the state level, it was a signal of hope for future data-privacy rights. By 1970, Germany had a decades-long history of having its people's personal data exploited. Access to personal data systems played a huge role in Nazi Germany's genocide of six million Jews during the Holocaust.[18] Government data was one piece of the puzzle, but data was exploited wherever it could be found.

In 1939, Germany's census included expanded questions about individuals' religious background. The survey asked about residents' religious affiliation, as prior German censuses had, but this time the survey also requested information on the religious background of each individual's grandparents. The German Statistical Office used that data to create categories of "racial Jews," and any information pertaining to a person's Jewish ancestry had to be recorded on a supplementary card.[19]

The supplementary cards weren't the government's primary source in targeting Jewish populations, although some individuals' unprotected personal data did make it into the wrong hands and aided the Nazi party's genocidal mission. In all, historians and statisticians noted three distinct data sources for the deportation lists: a monthly canvass of the Jewish population that the Gestapo (the state secret police) ordered Jewish community organizations to carry out; the Gestapo card file of Jews based on unprotected personal data from the 1939 census; and a mix of police records, Jewish community organization tax and housing records, and card files of ghetto residents maintained by community organizations.[20] Personal data was misused throughout Europe for similar purposes, including in Poland, France, the Netherlands, and Norway.[21]

Many other population groups were targeted in Europe during the Holocaust. Nazis accessed personal data in the genocide of psychiatric patients, the physically disabled, people suspected of homosexuality, and the Roma population (historically referred to as "gypsies"), among others.[22] For example, it's estimated that between 220,000 and 269,500 individuals with schizophrenia were sterilized or killed during the war.[23] The victims were targeted through information that the directors of all German psychiatric hospitals were asked to share regarding the diagnosis and capacity for useful work of each of their patients. When instructed to fill out forms containing this data, the directors were not told how the forms would be used.[24]

Unfortunately, the atrocities in Europe during World War II were not the only time personal data systems were exploited to abuse population groups. Instances of genocide and forced migration have occurred throughout history, including the internment of Japanese Americans during that same period; the forced removal of Native Americans from their territorial lands in the United States in the nineteenth century; the forced migration of minority populations in the Soviet Union in the 1920s and 1930s; and the Rwandan genocide of 1994.[25] Researchers have found that each of these events can be linked to misused personal data.

In Europe, abuse of personal information did not end with the war. When Germany led the way with the world's first data-protection act in 1970, East Germans had endured two decades of surveillance under the Ministry for State Security, also known as the Stasi. This secret police force's activities weren't monitored or regulated, and the force only answered to the Socialist Unity Party of Germany. East Germans' privacy was regularly violated under Stasi surveillance. At any time, their phone could be bugged or their intimate, personal lives spied upon. Citizens were vulnerable to violent and arbitrary arrests if there was any suspicion by the Stasi that a person was a danger to the ruling regime.[26] While the Hessian Data Protection Act only benefited people in the West German state of Hesse, the Stasi's abuse of power in the East showed what could happen when individuals' personal information was not protected. With Hesse's example at the helm, other European countries continued to lead the way. The Swedish Data Act became the first piece of nationwide legislation designed to protect citizens' personal data in 1973, and federal data-protection laws went into effect in Germany, France, and the United Kingdom over the next decade.[27] Europe understood intimately what could happen if personal data got into the wrong hands. That experience has turned European countries into the world's leaders in defending personal data, and they continue to lead the charge today.

It All Comes Full Circle

Even if we feel we have nothing to hide, we all still have an expectation of privacy. This may look like a teenager placing a "Private: Keep Out" sign on their bedroom door to prevent a sibling intrusion, an individual trusting that they can attend a therapy session without notes being made public, or someone feeling secure that they can bank online without their account details being shared. We all value privacy and have a right to our data being protected.

If you're ever looking for a sign of the times, data-privacy laws are a great indicator. The privacy landscape is a direct reaction to evolving technology and cultural perspectives. Today's data-privacy laws are centered around how companies can collect personal information, what kind of consent they need before they can collect it, how it should be handled once they have it, and how it can be shared. Most laws also give individuals (a.k.a. data subjects) the right to request that companies share what personal information any company may store about them.

Laws are this comprehensive today because our daily activities make it easy for others to access *so much* of our personal data. Most of that activity is on the internet, but these laws apply to anything we do—whether we're exchanging Instagram DMs, signing a print copy of a rental agreement for a new apartment, or collecting emails on a clipboard at a mall kiosk.

When you consider just how much we do online, from shopping and banking to sharing photos and researching sensitive topics, it's more critical than ever that our private information remains private. In essence, our computers and smartphones have become our castle, and without regulations in place that protect our right to privacy, others can listen to what we're doing on the other side of the wall. Our need for privacy hasn't really changed over time. It's just that our culture, technology, and behavior have, and we need privacy laws to evolve with them. The good news is, as you'll learn in the chapters ahead, the laws *are* evolving.

TL;DR CHEAT SHEET

- Privacy rights are human rights and date back to seventeenth century English common law and the Castle Doctrine, granting individuals the right to a safe, personal space.
- The advent of the printing press ignited civilian concerns about having personal business and images printed for public consumption without consent.
- The European Union's General Data Protection Regulation (GDPR) has become the template for many national, state, and industry-based privacy regulations.
- The EU based the GDPR in part on lessons learned from WWII, specifically Germany's exploitation of census data in persecuting and killing Jews and community and police data to target people with mental illnesses, physical disabilities, and minority sexual orientations.
- Access to personal data was also exploited globally throughout history, including the internment of Japanese Americans during WWII, the forced removal of Native Americans from their land in the nineteenth century, the forced migration of minority populations in the Soviet Union in the 1920s and 1930s, and the Rwandan genocide of 1994.
- We all have a right to privacy, whether we're a teenager putting a "Keep Out" sign on our bedroom door, a patient accessing mental health or other medical treatment, or someone banking and shopping online.
- Our digital footprints and our devices have now become our castles.

CHAPTER 2

How Our Data Gets into So Many Hands

Anyone helping to build a privacy program for their company sits on both sides of the data equation: They're part of a business that collects personal data, whatever their role in that process may be. They're also data subjects (both in- and outside of work) whose personal data is collected, shared, and processed nearly every time they open an internet browser. You're likely one of those people since you're reading this book. It's a great perspective to have as you develop data-handling practices within your company that focus on doing the right thing and building trust with customers. As you build your privacy program, you can do a gut check by asking, "How would I like it if a company accessed, handled, or shared my data in the way that my company is planning to do it?"

Part 2 walks you through the steps to develop your program.

Before we roll up our sleeves to create a privacy program, it helps to understand how consumer data is collected and how it's become so easy for others to access personal data that we never intended to share with them. These facts help us see that having a strong data-privacy program isn't just about checking a compliance box; it's about helping to protect consumers' fundamental right to privacy.

We Agree to More than We May Think

Most of us don't realize just how much of our personal data is available to others. What's often even more surprising is that we've given our consent for that data to be collected, stored, and shared. But it goes further than that. Technologies can piece together our data points to extrapolate information about us that we haven't shared. They can figure out what we're shopping for, our future shopping needs, when we're expecting a baby, when we're on the brink of a divorce . . . the possibilities are endless. And it's all (usually, sort of) legal.

There is so much opportunity to profit from personal data that a whole industry now exists dedicated to mining and brokering it. Some companies that started out as something entirely different have pivoted to making most of their money selling data. Remember the location check-in app Foursquare? They were wildly successful in the early 2010s as folks got hooked on earning badges and sharing their location with friends. After their success in the consumer space, they began selling their location-sharing technology and data to companies like Uber, Spotify, and JetBlue.[28] And they're not alone. The data broker market was valued at $280 billion in 2023, and total data broker revenue is expected to grow at a compound annual rate of 4.5 percent by 2030, reaching over $382 billion.[29]

Increased scrutiny on data brokering and advertising business models is pushing change, such as the Delete Act in California, which goes into effect in 2026. The law will allow consumers to make a single request that requires every data broker that maintains any personal information about them to delete that information.[30] Other US states are following with similar laws, but it will be some time before consumer rights surrounding data brokers become ubiquitous. Until that happens, it's important that anyone who has set out to build a strong data-privacy program understands how we got here. How did our data become so accessible (often without our realizing it) that it fuels a multibillion-dollar industry?

Well, two reasons: 1. Tech developers are famously fast, and 2. Lawmakers are notoriously slow. Once tech existed that made it possible to collect data, it evolved exponentially and became cheap (even free). Then, lots of smart people figured out how to monetize that data. The tech kept evolving, smart people kept optimizing data monetization, and the industry took off.

At first, there were very few regulations in place to restrict how data could be used. That meant app owners technically weren't doing anything wrong when they, for example, collected your location information and sold it to a third party—even when your location wasn't needed for you to use their app. They just collected the data because they could and because there was probably a way to exploit it somehow, at some point. And the layers run deeper. Most developers build their apps using a software development kit (SDK), which is a collection of programs bundled into one installable package. App developers often don't realize that some of those SDKs supply data brokers with their end users' data.[31] This means personal data may be leaking out through SDK providers without the app developer or the app's end user knowing about it. Apps are only one example. As you'll see, our data is constantly collected, passed on, and leveraged for profit virtually any time we open a web browser.

It's great news that the public finally has some protection under new privacy regulations, and that protection will grow in the not-too-distant future. But the opacity at play raises alarm bells for companies that may not realize how much of their end users' information they're actually sharing. And with that, whether the third parties brokering that data are putting them in a potential position of noncompliance. A hint: they can be. Companies also need to consider whether their own data-handling processes are violating any current or upcoming privacy regulations. It's a complicated web of cause and effect that can feel impossible to untangle—but it is possible. And, as problematic as this situation may seem, it doesn't mean you need to ditch all of the tech you rely on to run your business.

I'll walk you through the solutions to this great data dilemma in the chapters ahead. But before we try to solve the problem, it's important to understand what's even happening and how we got here. To do that, let's start at the beginning, in an ancient period known as the 1990s.

The Quest for Our Data

Much of our data is collected through our web browsing activity, so it helps to know how that's even possible.

I won't bore you with the technical details of how the internet works. For now, it's enough to know that every website and its related data are stored on a web server. Just like you might save files locally on your computer's hard drive, websites are collections of files stored on servers that are hosted on physical computers. If you've never seen one before, do an image search for "data server farm" to see how the world's data is stored. It's fascinating. All digital content has a physical footprint of some kind.

The first website was created in 1991 by British computer scientist

Tim Berners-Lee,* and he hosted the site on his NeXT com-
puter.³² That's how it worked in the early days. If you wanted
a website, you had to host it on a computer and server that you owned
or at least had access to. You also had to buy whatever software
was needed to create and publish your site or hire a developer
to do it for you (the more likely option). That bundle of components
all working together—from your server to your software—was your
technology stack.

Free web-hosting companies like Angelfire, GeoCities, and Tripod
entered the scene in 1995, and if you're old enough to remember the '90s, you'll recall that websites made on those platforms
weren't very appealing. So, most website owners continued hosting
and creating sites themselves. Server space was expensive, and building a website was infinitely harder than it is today, but it was great
from a privacy standpoint. Since you owned and operated your site
locally, you interacted directly with your website visitors, and you were
the only one with access to any data related to your site.

Now, let's zero in on that last piece: the data related to your site.

The other basic thing you need to know about how the internet works, if you want to understand the origins of data sharing,
is *how stuff communicates across the web*. TCP/IP is the standard
form of communication between devices connected to the internet.**
You are probably familiar with the "IP" part of TCP/IP. Anything with
an online connection has an IP address, from your smartwatch, ther-
mostat, or baby monitor to your computer. And every website is linked
to the IP address of the computer that hosts its server.

To keep it simple, TCP/IP is a set of protocols that specify how

---

* If you're curious, the first website is still accessible at its original URL: http://
info.cern.ch/hypertext/WWW/TheProject.html.

** Which, if you're interested, stands for Transmission Control Protocol/
Internet Protocol.

devices exchange data over the internet with one another. One of the most common TCP/IP protocols is HTTP,*** which handles the communication between a web server and a web browser.[33]

Here's where your data comes into play. Virtually all web servers create server logs, which are text documents containing a record of the activity related to that server. When you type a URL into your browser or search for keywords and then click through to a website, your browser makes a request to that website's server to deliver whatever page you're looking for. Imagine it like an old-fashioned phone exchange, where you are calling the operator and asking them to connect you to a specific phone line. In this context, the operator is the server, and you're asking the server to connect you to a specific website that it hosts. Your request includes a bunch of information about you, like your device's IP address, your location, the type of device you're using, the date and time you visited the site, the search terms you used to find the site, and more.[34] All that data gets stored on the website's server in an HTTP log.

In the early days, if a website owner wanted to understand how people used their site, they had to buy software that would parse their server logs. That's the only way they could access important data like what path a user took to get to a page, which pages were the most popular, how many visitors they had, where those visitors were from, and anything else their log server captured. That software was pretty expensive and difficult to administer, so most website owners at the time skipped it and remained clueless about how users interacted with their sites. But that didn't last long.

By the mid-'90s, free website analytics software began to emerge in the form of "hit counters." You probably remember them if you were around during the dawn of the web. They were basic

---

*** Short for Hypertext Transfer Protocol.

counters at the bottom of a website that showed how many visitors a site received. They don't hold a candle to modern web analytics tools, but back then, they were groundbreaking. Hit counters were some of the first free, user-friendly web analytics tools available, and they gave website owners an early taste of how useful it can be to know how users interact with their websites. They were also super timely, since the key metric advertisers and investors cared about back then were eyeballs. From the mid-'90s to around the early 2000s, ad revenue mostly came through display ads, and success was measured by the number of views an ad received.

For a while, website counters remained the main form of analytics available on a mass scale. It was still expensive to get your server logs analyzed, and even just storing logs was becoming more costly as the internet gained popularity (because higher traffic = more activity = larger server logs). The only other viable option for user insights was to pay for display ads to appear across a range of websites and measure how many views your ads received. But this was the mid-'90s. While data access was limited for that blip of time, many brilliant developers were crafting solutions behind the scenes.

Two companies launched in 1995 that had a big impact on the world of personal data: Urchin, which Google bought in 2005, and DoubleClick, which Google bought in 2008.

Urchin was one of the first free analytics tools that gave website owners insight about their users beyond a basic counter. It tapped into server logs to provide user-specific data like how a person came to the site (i.e., referrers), when they visited, user location, and user authentication. Until this point, that sort of data was mostly only available to large enterprises that could afford log-analyzing software. Urchin was one of those expensive options until it launched its free version, Urchin ASAP, which was funded by revenue from display ads. The software kept evolving until the company hit a major breakthrough: it developed the first analytics tool to combine data mined from server logs with data collected via tags (i.e., snippets of code on a website that collect user data) so that unique visitors could be established and tracked.[35]

Now website owners could identify unique visitors; click paths; and return-loyalty metrics, like whether someone is a first-time visitor, a returning visitor, and how frequently they visit a site.[36] This was huge for sales and marketing. Suddenly, you could know who was visiting your site and what they wanted—and you could adjust your efforts accordingly.

It turns out that two parallel-but-related industries were evolving quickly in the late '90s and early 2000s: web analytics and online advertising. Both exploded because folks were waking up to the idea that there is tremendous value in knowing what individuals are doing online. While website visitors could not be personally identified (and they still can't be today, per privacy regulations), it's valuable to know how each visitor interacts with a site. And developers were constantly figuring out new ways to deliver that specific user data to website owners and advertisers.

As Urchin upended the web-analytics world, DoubleClick was doing the same in the ad world. Its main contribution was its DART tool, which used third-party cookies (more on first- vs. third-party cookies in a minute) to track individuals' web browsing activity across multiple websites and then leveraged that data to serve people targeted ads. This approach was immediately embraced by advertisers and questioned by those who were aware of how DoubleClick operated. DoubleClick caused such a stir that the *New York Times* published a profile on it in 1999 called "An Advertising Power, but Just What Does DoubleClick Do?"[37] The article noted that DoubleClick had evolved into a multinational corporation with 660 employees and more than three thousand advertising clients within four years of its founding by two Atlanta engineers.

Barry Salzman, the president of DoubleClick's international

division at the time, explained to the *Times* that the company's approach could "get the right advertisement to the right person at the right time." This was an epic promise in the advertising world, where understanding whether expensive ads actually succeeded in attracting customers was a perpetual challenge. When using DoubleClick, Salzman shared that an advertiser can say, for example, that they only want to reach businesspeople in the financial industry who live in New York City and ski, and they only want to reach them between nine and five. DoubleClick could deliver ads to them and only them.[38] With powers like that, advertisers were happy to hand over 35 to 50 percent of their advertising income to DoubleClick.

These developments were a boon for anyone trying to make money online—and they were built entirely on web visitors' personal data. That's fine, and remember, it's the basic deal we agree to when we use the internet. We get free content, and in exchange, we allow websites to collect data about our online activity. But the lines between right and wrong got fuzzy fast as developers found new ways to leverage data they collected by tracking people across multiple websites. By 2000, the Federal Trade Commission (FTC) and the New York attorney general's office had each launched investigations on DoubleClick in response to privacy concerns. The company was also the target of six private lawsuits involving its web-privacy practices.[39] The FTC closed its investigation in early 2001, citing no foul play.[40] But the New York attorney general's office came to a settlement with DoubleClick that required the company to make its tracking activities more visible and give consumers access to their online profiles. They also had to pay $450K in settlement costs.[41]

DoubleClick's trajectory was only one part of the big-data land grab that was taking shape. As the century turned, tag-based marketing integrations were becoming more ubiquitous. This means that analytics and advertising tools didn't even need to access server logs to obtain user data anymore. They just needed to drop a small amount of code into each page of a website. This made data collection easier than ever—and there were still very few regulations in place to slow down innovations in the space.

Meanwhile, every corner of the internet was evolving. Cloud computing was gaining momentum as platforms like Salesforce launched in 1999, giving companies cloud-based customer management tools for the first time. That same year also brought us free web-based blogging platforms like LiveJournal and Blogger, and affordable options for website hosting were becoming plentiful. All these developments led to a big shift away from websites and other digital products being hosted on private servers and toward those sites being built on top of third-party platforms. Those platforms were largely secure, but the fact remained that now website data wasn't exclusive to logs that were locked away on servers. It was accessible to third-party platforms—for better or worse. And as data collection and sharing evolved faster than regulations could keep up with, there was no clear way to find out who had our data or how it was being used.

We All Started Out with Good Intentions

It may be hard to believe, but the tech behind some of today's most questionable data-handling practices was created with good intentions. Take cookies. They're often blamed as a key cause for our data-privacy concerns, but cookies themselves are not the problem. The issues arise out of the creative, and arguably unethical, ways that some developers have used certain cookies to track people's web-surfing activity.

Before we dig into how and why this is, let's look at why cookies exist in the first place. They were invented in 1994 by the internet browser Netscape as a way for websites to remember basic visitor information. This was a huge development, and we still rely on cookies today for an optimal web-browsing experience.

The way cookies work is pretty simple: they are small text files that a website stores on your computer via your browser. By themselves, cookies don't do anything; they just store information that the website can read later to perform some kind of function. Every time you go to that site in the future, the cookie alerts the site that you've been there before and tailors your subsequent visits accordingly. Cookies allow a website to maintain your preferences, like your preferred language or your stored username and password. They're also how Amazon knows what products you might like; how YouTube knows your favorite channels; how a game you're playing knows what levels you've already completed; and how you can fill a shopping cart, leave the page, and come back to find your stuff is still in the cart.

At this point in our evolution as internet users, we'd be pretty annoyed by our experience if a site *didn't* use cookies to remember us. All that efficiency would be gone.

It's important to understand that there are two kinds of cookies: **first-party** and **third-party cookies**.

First-party cookies are the ones set by the website you've visited. Most (but not all) are necessary for efficient website functionality, which is why first-party cookies are often referred to as "essential cookies." Their core purpose is to remember visitors in the ways just described to create an efficient web-browsing experience. First-party cookies also help the website owner by collecting user data, much like server logs do.

Third-party cookies, often called "nonessential cookies," are a bit different. These are set by another website than the one you visited. Advertising networks like DoubleClick are a great example of this. If a brand wants to advertise its products, it might add some code from an advertising network to its website. That code drops a cookie on your browser when you visit the brand's website. Even though you were visiting the brand's website, the cookie itself comes from the advertiser (i.e., a third party). So long as you have that cookie on your browser, if you visit another website that displays ads from the advertiser, you'll see ads related to the brand whose website you initially visited.

Some major internet browsers, like Google Chrome, are phasing out third-party cookies, but there are more ways to track people's web-browsing activity. Another tracking device called a **pixel** is a 1x1 transparent image embedded in a website, email, or ad that contains a link to an external server. When a user interacts with that content, their browser downloads the pixel. The user has no idea they've downloaded the pixel, but nonetheless, that action sends a bunch of data about them to the pixel server, such as who downloaded the pixel, their operating system, the type of browser they used, a time stamp for the interaction, the user's IP address, and more. Pixels are sometimes used as work-arounds for cookie-blocking tools.

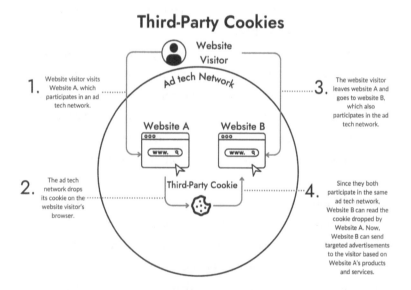

Third-Party Cookies

Website Visitor

Ad tech Network

1. Website visitor visits Website A, which participates in an ad tech network.

2. The ad tech network drops its cookie on the website visitor's browser.

3. The website visitor leaves website A and goes to website B, which also participates in the ad tech network.

4. Since they both participate in the same ad tech network, Website B can read the cookie dropped by Website A. Now, Website B can send targeted advertisements to the visitor based on Website A's products and services.

Website A

Website B

Third-Party Cookie

Whatever tracking device is being used, **tags** are the key vehicle that makes it possible. Tags are small segments of code that execute when loading a website. There's a lot of overlap between tags and cookies and pixels. Cookies and pixels are typically set by tags.

There's more to the tech, of course, but that's about all you need to know from a data-privacy standpoint.

Once we realize all of the questionable ways in which tracking tools

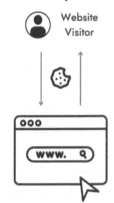

First-Party Cookies

Website Visitor

Website drops a first-party cookie to identify the visitor when they return.

are used today, it can be surprising to learn that they were not created with malicious intent. When they were invented, everyone was just trying to build a better internet. Cookies were created so that we could have a better web-browsing experience. Then tag-based tracking across websites emerged so that advertising could be more effective and efficient. Media analyst Thomas Baekdal even notes that the original specification for how cookies should be implemented in browsers, created in 1997 and revised in 2000, was actually GDPR compliant.[42] It did not allow for third-party tracking without the user's explicit and active consent, which is a big part of GDPR's guidelines today.

The problem was that the specifications were ignored, and with minimal regulations in place to stop developers from creating tag-based tracking tools that drove revenue, the tech just kept evolving. But even still—despite the internet being a modern-day Wild West in the '90s and early 2000s—companies were trying to be ethical. Especially those, like Google, that had big plans for world domination.

Don't Be Evil

For nearly two decades, Google's unofficial motto was Don't Be Evil. They adopted it in the late '90s as the company was figuring out how to grow its revenue. At the time, Google was a fledgling startup with one income source: licensing search. Website owners would pay to have Google's search capabilities installed on their site so that visitors could easily search their content.[43] It was a natural move since Google's core goal back then was to organize the world's information.

But licensing search could only get them so far. If Google was going to become the giant that it aspired to be, the company needed to find more ways to monetize the business. Founders Larry Page and Sergey Brin had decided early on that they wanted Google to be free for users. That left them with advertisers as their key customer base. Google executives knew there was major potential in monetizing the one thing website owners cared about most in those days: eyeballs.

Google engineers Paul Buchheit and Amit Patel are often credited for coming up with Don't Be Evil when their colleagues were just starting to build advertising partnerships. They worried that monetizing search results would compromise the company's integrity if they promised ad partners that they'd appear at the top of search results. That's not the kind of business they were running. They wanted to optimize for revenue without jeopardizing their users' trust or happiness.

In an interview with *Vox*, early Google executive Marissa Mayer recalls that Patel wrote the phrase Don't Be Evil on the conference room whiteboard where Google team members were about to have a business meeting with the *Washington Post*.[44] It was the North Star they needed as they navigated the new world of monetizing search.

Later, Buchheit suggested making the phrase part of Google's official code of conduct. And it stuck. Don't Be Evil was at the top of the company's code of conduct until 2018, when it quietly moved the motto way down to the bottom. *Why* they moved it out of the spotlight is a bit of a mystery, and we can never know the whole story. It was a company-wide value, after all, so it applied to internal company dynamics as well as to how they served the public. Yet even if we *only* look at some of Google's customer-facing activities, we can see how a mantra as pointed as Don't Be Evil would become complicated to follow as search, advertising, and analytics continued to grow and intersect.

When Forces Combine

Google's answer to their revenue puzzle was to launch AdWords in 2000. It was the internet's first self-serve online advertising platform and the foundation upon which Google built its advertising empire. The AdWords model revolved around eyeballs: Website owners would pay to have their text ad appear alongside search results that used keywords relevant to the advertiser's site. It was a simple way to boost your page's visibility on the new search engine that had already become a household name. And for Google, it was the answer to monetizing the company's service, sans evil. Ads were visually different from search results, which remained organic.

Back then, evading evil with AdWords seemed simple enough. Google mainly had to make sure it didn't let advertising revenue compromise the integrity of its search results.[45] But complexity crept in as Google added new features, and the definition of *evil* became more and more subjective.

A major turning point was Google's purchase of Urchin in 2005. Remember, as Google focused on organizing the world's information in the late '90s into the 2000s, Urchin was hard at work optimizing web analytics. When the two companies joined forces, magic ensued. It was a case of one plus one equaling much more than two.

Google relaunched Urchin On-Demand, which previously

had a $500 a month price tag, as Google Analytics (GA). With that, the world's most robust, free data analytics tool was born. Brian Clifton, Google's head of web analytics for Europe at the time, recalled that the impact of making analytics free was dramatic. "An industry that once counted its customers in the tens of thousands, now exploded," he noted. "In fact, so dramatic was the uptake of the service that it had to close to new subscribers for 10 months while new machines were allocated to the number-crunching tasks at Google's data centers." Once reopened, Google Analytics' user base surpassed a million in a matter of months.[46]

Google took the leap to make GA free because the company anticipated it would increase the AdWords revenue. Clifton explained the logic behind the free business model, saying that it provided accountability and transparency to existing Google advertisers. It also proved the value of online advertising to potential new advertisers. Clifton wrote about the strategy in 2007, explaining that "for Google, maybe as a result of using Google Analytics, customers will remain advertisers for a longer period, become less likely to lapse their accounts (take breaks from advertising), even raise their AdWords budgets to capture a greater share of the search market. For those users that are not advertisers, perhaps Google Analytics will give them the confidence to try it."[47]

Google built its analytics tool right into AdWords. The company introduced it on the *Inside AdWords* blog by telling advertisers that it "tells you everything you want to know about how your visitors found you and how they interact with your site. It will track all of your online campaigns, from emails to keywords, regardless of search engine or referral source." Advertisers just had to add a few lines of tracking code to each page of their websites and they had full access to their web analytics reports.[48]

Google's bet on free worked, of course. Total revenue jumped from $6.1 billion in 2005 to $10.6 billion in 2006, the first full year with

GA.[49] In 2007, there was $16.6 billion in revenue, with advertising being 99 percent of the revenue source each of those years.[50] Everyone was winning. Advertisers clearly saw value in knowing how people interacted with their content and ad campaigns, and Google had cracked the code on a seemingly open-ended revenue source. Now, they wanted more.

Google closed the first quarter of 2008 by buying DoubleClick. The company saw so much potential in this expansion to its advertising platform that CEO Eric Schmidt mentioned it with the release of the 2008 Q1 financial results. "Our ongoing innovation in search, ads, and apps helped drive healthy growth globally across our product lines," he said. "As we integrate DoubleClick into our advertising platform, we see exciting new ways to improve the user experience and increase value for our advertisers and partners."[51]

The goal was still to create a better internet for all, but as key innovations relied more and more on user data, the complexities kept coming. Remember, DoubleClick had faced privacy lawsuits as early as 2000, when its influence was relatively microscopic compared to the reach it would have under Google. Folks were already concerned that advertisers had insight on their web activity across websites. But now Google had access to that information too. So it was no longer just that Patagonia knew I saw its ad on DSW .com, FootLocker.com, and Zappos.com and adjusted my ad-viewing experience accordingly. Now Google knew I'd been shopping for basketball shoes because that's what I searched for when visiting those sites. Suddenly I started seeing ads for Air Jordans on sale at Nike .com when I scrolled through Facebook because Google told Facebook that's what I was looking for. That means Nike wins a little, too, because it got to target me with an ad for something it knew I wanted. And Google wins because it further developed its advertising relationship with Nike. And, well, I win too because now I know Jordans are on sale at Nike.com. Everyone's happy, right? Maybe.

This all could be fine when we're just searching for shoes. The challenge is that developers kept finding new ways to collect user information across websites through things like forms, chat widgets, and so on. And data brokers kept coming up with new ways to process user data. That was the beginning of the slippery slope of data sharing without user consent that we're still navigating today.

The Lucrative Quest to Figure Out Who You Are

If there's any concern that Google may have given up on its Don't Be Evil mantra, what about the people and companies who never made that sort of promise at all? Digital businesses and data brokers have an ongoing goal: to make a profit off of your personal information. Firms are highly incentivized to figure out who you are and what you're interested in because well-targeted ads bring in the most money.

For this to work, your attention is the most valuable commodity. When an approach is no longer optimal—because, say, new tech has managed to block it—firms just need to find a new one. And so far in internet history, there have *always* been new ways to collect and exploit personal data, with no obligations for anyone to follow any sort of moral code. We likely won't know every tactic that's ever been used, but it's important to understand some of the ways our data is swiped without our consent, and even without cookies and pixels. From a compliance standpoint, many companies are shocked to discover the liberties that ad tech businesses take with their visitors' personal data. Even more surprising is this: the advertisers could be held accountable for actions they don't even know are happening. Here are some key ways data is swiped without consent.

Browser fingerprinting: As browsers started implementing cookie-blocking settings, businesses realized they don't even need cookies to identify unique website visitors. They can get all the information they need through **browser fingerprinting**. The evil genius behind this method is that it combines basic information that's accessible through server logs with other nonpersonal details about a website visitor that are acquired by running some simple script on a website. When every little detail is combined, it creates a hyper-specific profile about a web visitor that can then be tracked.

The key piece of identifying information in server logs is the **user agent string**. It includes details about the visitor's browser and device that help the website know what content to serve to that visitor and in what format. If you're visiting a site from Safari on an iPad running iPadOS 15, the agent string notes this and the website will serve their content to you in a format that's different from what they'd send to a visitor whose agent string shows they're using Firefox on Windows 11. Separately, websites can run scripts that gather more detail about a user, like what fonts, plug-ins, and cookies they have installed; their preferred language; their time zone, screen size, and keyboard layout; their browser permission settings; and much more.

Each individual bit of data doesn't say much, but when they're combined into a single user profile, the likelihood that anyone else will have the exact same data profile is so rare that it ends up creating an incredibly unique signature. That means a business can identify you in a crowd of a hundred thousand people by simply seeing your browser again, even if they've never dropped a cookie into that browser, and they can then track your online activity. So, for example, if an ad broker sees that someone with your browser fingerprint was shopping for fly-fishing rods at Cabela's, and then a short while later someone with that same browser fingerprint was searching for waders at Bass Pro Shops, it can infer that you're the same person and that you're going fly-fishing soon. Now they know to target you with fly-fishing-related ads, even if you've never consented to sharing your data with them.

The good news is that browsers have been fighting back against fingerprinting over the last few years. Brave was one of the first browsers to implement antifingerprint technology, and others like Safari and Chrome have followed. The result is that most of the ad tech that relied on fingerprinting will soon be obsolete if it isn't already, but it's still important for internet users to be aware of fingerprinting and how it works.

Tracking home IP addresses: This is another way that marketers have managed to track user data without cookies or consent. Big ad agencies and data brokers leverage it heavily since they can make lots of useful inferences about someone just by knowing their IP address. It wasn't an issue in the early internet days, when a user's IP address would change every time they dialed in to catch an internet connection (cue the '90s' *eeeee ooooo eeeee you've got mail!*, for those who were around for it). Today, since we're all on cable modems or fiber, our IP addresses rarely change. The result is that data trackers can take note of when your IP address shows up in server logs across the web and make inferences about you through your browsing history. They can't figure out who you are specifically, but they can get information that's *good enough* for their purposes. So they may see that, in addition to the fly-fishing gear you shopped for, you also bought pink toddler sneakers on Zappos.com, watched some videos on DIY deck repairs, and bought a family pass to an amusement park in Boise, Idaho. They also have a sense of your general location through your IP address, and they can do a reverse lookup on your IP address to see that it's coming from a broadband provider, confirming that it's a home IP address.

Based on that set of information alone, they can infer that you're likely a homeowner and a parent in the Boise area who is interested in fly-fishing and family activities. It's not as valuable as if you were personally identified, but it's definitely enough information for an ad company to start targeting you.

Browsers have been fighting back against this too, with tools that hide your IP address, like Apple's Private Relay. Several other browsers have similar built-in tracking blockers.

Geotargeting: This tracking method requires user interaction, but it's still nefarious when used to its full capacity. You know how some websites ask for permission to know your location? It's usually so they can deliver something useful to you, like directions to their office or store, so it seems reasonable to click "Yes." You're getting value in exchange for sharing your information. The problem is, a number of ad tech firms exploit visitors' consent to share their location and use it to derive a surprising amount of personal data about them.

Most people don't realize that when they click "Yes," the location they're sharing is accurate to within a few meters. As in, those companies can tell where you are *in your house* to a scary degree of accuracy. And they can do a lot with that data. Let's say you're searching for dentists in the Austin, Texas, area. You go to a practice's website and agree to share your location so you can see where their office is in relation to your house. The data trackers on that site already had access to your IP address, and now that they know your exact location, they can confirm it's a home IP address. They can also do a reverse lookup on the latitude and longitude of your location to find your mailing address and start sending you direct mail related to dentists in Austin. They can do a reverse lookup on the property's tax rolls to pull the homeowner's name. And if you're that homeowner, they now know who you are. If you co-own, they know who that person is too. All of this happened just because you clicked "Yes" on a location prompt thinking you were getting some value from it.

This list is not exhaustive. Ad-tech firms are constantly finding new ways to pull your personal data. Once they have it, data brokers take things to the next level by aggregating bits of data that have been pulled from various sources and merging them into hyper-specific user profiles. Then they sell lists containing people's personal data to nearly anyone who is willing to pay for them.

Most consumers don't worry much about this because they either don't know it's happening or they don't see the harm. What's the big deal if Zappos knows you're searching for toddler dress shoes or a dentist office in your area knows you're looking to switch practices, right? Well, the first problem is the lack of transparency. Personal data is too often collected through trickery when folks consent to share their data for one purpose and then it's used for another. But also, the details of your life can be pulled and combined enough for firms to know deeply personal information about you, like your medical history, whether you've visited an abortion clinic, or whether you're struggling with consumer debt. Perhaps you still don't see the harm in that if you feel you have nothing to hide. If that's the case, you may change your mind when you realize that advertisers are not the only ones with access to that personal data. Nearly anyone who wants to know more about who you are, what you're doing, and where they can find you can buy data from brokers to learn what they want about you, from ex-partners to governments.

We Can Be Part of the Change

As a business, it can feel nearly impossible to protect customer data with so many outside factors working against us. Even if our company doesn't exchange data with brokers, how can we be sure our vendors and partners don't take liberties with the data they access through us? The challenge can seem even more daunting if your company *does* exchange data with brokers for any reason.

Fortunately, times are changing for the better. Now more than ever, it's possible to benefit from user data *and* protect it from getting into the wrong hands. We don't have to choose. We can do both. You'll see exactly how to do that as you develop your privacy program using this book as your guide.

TL;DR CHEAT SHEET

- Gut check: "How would I like it if a company accessed, handled, or shared my data in the way that my company is planning to?"
- Consumer data has been so accessible because tech developers are fast and lawmakers are slow—there's a policy lag.
- Data brokers aggregate consumer data and sell it to companies. This largely unregulated industry is experiencing projected compound annual growth of 4.5 percent by 2030, reaching over $382 billion.
- Cookies are the most widely used tool for tracking user behavior and collecting data.
- First-party cookies are small text files that a website stores on a computer via internet browsers to perform certain functions. This is how a website "remembers" a visitor's preferred language, how Amazon knows the products a customer likes, how a game knows the levels a player has completed, or how a web store still has a visitor's products in their shopping cart when they close the page and come back later.
- Third-party cookies track users across websites. They enable what we now call retargeting ads, where you search for Air Jordans via Google on your lunch break and are served a Nike ad about Air Jordan sales when you scroll Instagram later that night.
- Cookies, pixels, and tags are all ways to track consumer behavior legally. There are various other methods too, such as browser fingerprinting, tracking home IP addresses, and geotargeting, some of which are more questionable than others.

CHAPTER 3

Why We Should Care about What the Government Knows about Us

S ome of our biggest concerns around data privacy have nothing to do with advertising. Most individuals are not worried that a company will do such a good job of targeting advertisements to us that we'll buy gadgets we didn't plan on or a Caribbean vacation outside our budget just because an ad reached us at the exact right moment. The core problem is the lack of transparency. We usually have no idea how much of our data is mined, who has access to it, what's being done with it, or how those activities affect our lives. Even if we diligently read every privacy policy we accept (and who does?), we typically don't know what companies and data brokers will do with our information once they have it.

This applies to much more than our web browsing activity and app usage. We can generate traceable, personal data any time we drive a car, visit a healthcare provider, text a friend, make a purchase, or just walk down the street. We can even be identified based on data that *other* people put into the world.

Some of the most voracious consumers of all that personal data are governments seeking to monitor their people. This is a big deal, and more dangerous than it may seem. Governments can access and use our private data as a powerful weapon against us in ways we'd never imagine. The lack of transparency is one part of the problem. Most companies don't go out of their way to tell you, for example, that the government can access information like your emails, family photos, private messages, or phone location data. In fact, they can likely access any data an app holds about you: information on your menstrual cycle, daily routines, dating profile, exercise patterns, and even those questions we all ask search engines each time we get a sniffle. If an app stores data, the government can potentially access it.

There is also another peril at play: laws about how governments are allowed to access and use people's data can be vague—and at times nonexistent. That gives governments a surprising amount of leeway to rummage around in our private lives.

This is not alarmist thinking. It's been widely documented that governments have leveraged private data to violate human rights. As we covered in Chapter 1, national databases were a key resource in Nazi Germany's genocide of its Jewish population during World War II. Research has linked government misuse of personal data to other instances of genocide and forced migration throughout history, including Native Americans' forced removal from their territorial land in the United States in the nineteenth century and the 1994 Rwandan genocide.[52] In recent decades, China has accessed personal information to control, imprison, and commit other crimes against humanity against its Uyghur population.[53] And as technology develops, what may seem innovative or experimental can evolve into something different as social perceptions change.

Governments can legally monitor individuals' activities to varying degrees. China has tracked and controlled everything from how many children its citizens can birth to how many hours of video games those kids are allowed to play.[54] Russian law enforcement has used facial recognition technology to detain individuals suspected of evading the draft in the war on Ukraine.[55] In the United States, the Fourth Amendment can be interpreted to allow authorities to access individuals' private data with a warrant and then use that data to prosecute them. That's what happened to Mississippi mother of three Latice Fisher after she gave birth at home in 2018. It was reported that when EMTs arrived, the baby showed no signs of life and Fisher was brought to a local hospital. Court documents say that Fisher confided to a hospital nurse that she didn't want to be a mother again and had researched ways to terminate the pregnancy. Investigators accessed Fisher's cell phone memory and data to confirm that she had researched abortion medication during her pregnancy's third trimester. After authorities obtained that data alongside other evidence, Fisher was charged with second degree murder of her baby.[56] That evidence has since been challenged, and the charges were dropped.[57]

How governments can legally use our personal data against us is a divisive topic, no question. There are legitimate claims that data is necessary to stop terrorism, for example, but the problem runs deeper than that. Governments frequently find loopholes to source data that they may not be legally allowed to access by purchasing it from data brokers. This poses a frightening, open-ended threat to our privacy. Governments can simply buy their way to private information about us, ranging from our cell photo location records and online search history to aggregated data that pieces together details about our health, sexual orientation, or religious beliefs. They can figure out who we share a bed with, who our friends are, what we've purchased . . . the possibilities are limitless.

This can be a lot to take in, especially if you're already feeling overwhelmed by the challenges of keeping up and complying with privacy regulations. But you and I are not powerless. We may not have the authority to change governments' practices, but we can make sure we're not contributing to the problem if we take our role as data stewards seriously. We should protect data as if lives depend on its safekeeping, because sometimes they do. We can also take action to manage our own data, helping to set new consumer expectations and influence privacy norms. At Osano, we promote data minimization: the idea that you shouldn't take more data than you need and you should delete it when you're done with it. Yes, this helps with compliance, but it also helps reduce the potential risk of personal data being accessed and used in ways that can cause harm.

My goal in this chapter is to build awareness. The more we all know about how governments have accessed and misused our data, the more we can understand the urgency with which we must protect the data that's in our keeping. The pages ahead take a deeper dive into the topic. But the truth is, the examples here only scratch the surface of ways in which governments have accessed our data from private companies. There's also no knowing how data may potentially be accessed and misused in the future. All we can do is educate ourselves on what's happening—and acknowledge that we can't ever know *everything* that goes on once data leaves our hands. However, we can practice responsible data handling to ensure we're not part of the problem.

But I Have Nothing to Hide

"Why should I care? I have nothing to hide." This is the most common refrain I hear from audiences when I give talks about data privacy.

And it's understandable. We already know that the government has a bunch of information on us. Why should we be so alarmed that they can access more if they choose to? It stands to reason that if you've done nothing wrong, you have nothing to worry about.

Well, that's not entirely true. Innocent people have had their lives disrupted after being flagged for suspicious behavior and even wrongly accused of crimes based on their private data. The *New York Times* has reported on several cases in recent years in which Google's AI flagged users' content as suspicious. In one instance in 2021, Mark, a father in San Francisco, was locked out of his Google accounts days after he'd taken photos of his toddler son's genitalia to send to the family pediatrician as part of a telemedicine visit to diagnose an infection. Losing his Google accounts meant he couldn't access years of family photos, his email, his calendar, even his cell phone and contacts since he had an Android phone with a Google Fi plan.

Google also reported Mark to the San Francisco Police Department, who ran an investigation on him and obtained a warrant to access everything in Mark's Google account: his internet searches; his location history; his messages and any document, photo, or video he'd stored with the company.[58] After reviewing everything, the investigator determined that no crime had occurred and closed the case. But Google still refused to grant Mark access to his accounts. The *New York Times* reported that Mark eventually got six months of his Google data back, but not from Google. The police department gave it to him on a thumb drive, which they'd received from the company with a warrant.[59]

While losing his Google accounts was undoubtedly disruptive, Mark was lucky. False accusations connected to personal data have upended people's lives. In Avondale, Arizona, Jorge Molina was arrested and accused of murder in 2018 after Google location data indicated to police that he was at the crime scene when a murder happened. It wasn't true, but Molina spent six days in jail while his family presented evidence to police to prove his innocence. Charges were never pursued against Molina, although his arrest and jail time resulted in him having his car impounded, losing his job, dropping out of school, and experiencing severe psychological distress.[60] The mix-up occurred because someone close to Molina's family, who was at the crime scene and was eventually charged for the murder, was driving Molina's car at the time and using one of Molina's old cell phones, which was still logged into his Google accounts. ABC News reported that Google pegged Molina to the crime scene but also showed him in another location at the same time since his Google accounts were logged into multiple phones.[61] Two key data points convinced police that Molina was the suspect: his Google location information and video surveillance footage that showed shots were fired from a car that looked like the one Molina owned.

Law enforcement has used location data to successfully track criminals, but investigations often loop in innocent people and cause major anguish. Location data collected by the exercise-tracking app RunKeeper caused Zachary McCoy to be flagged as a suspect in a burglary that took place in the Florida neighborhood where he regularly rode his bike. He used the app to track his bike route, and the app shared that data with Google. McCoy discovered something was amiss when Google emailed him to let him know local police had requested that Google share information related to his account. He had no idea why law enforcement would be after him. Amidst his panic, he noticed a case number in Google's email and searched for it on the Gainesville Police Department's website. He got one result: an investigation report on a burglary in the neighborhood where he regularly biked. McCoy hired a lawyer to help deter law enforcement from accessing his personal data and convince them to drop their suspicions that he had anything to do with the crime.[62] If he hadn't brought in a lawyer, there is no knowing how far law enforcement would have gone in investigating McCoy.

The data trails that our phone and app usage generate are just one source of personal information that private companies may share with law enforcement. We can also get ensnared in government quandaries based on personal data they access that isn't even our own. New Orleans filmmaker Michael Usry Jr. became a suspect in the 1996 murder of Idaho teen Angie Dodge because his father's DNA was a partial match to DNA found at the crime scene. Usry Jr.'s father didn't fit the killer's profile, but Usry Jr. did. The *New Orleans Advocate* reported that once police investigated Michael Usry Jr., they became especially suspicious of him because films he'd created had recurring themes of murder and because they'd noticed that some of his Facebook friends lived in Idaho. Usry Jr. also had two sisters who attended a university about twenty-five miles from the crime scene.[63]

Police dropped their investigation of Usry Jr. after his own DNA sample wasn't a match to DNA found at the crime scene. But the path that led them to Usry Jr. in the first place demonstrates the surprising ways in which governments can use *other people's* personal data to track us down. In Usry Jr.'s case, the data trail started when Usry Jr.'s father took a DNA test years earlier for a church project. Those samples were sent to the Sorenson Molecular Genealogy Foundation, whose database was eventually acquired by Ancestry .com.[64] That means data on Usry Sr.'s DNA was now accessible through Ancestry.com. When investigators of the Angie Dodge murder case couldn't find a profile in the national law enforcement DNA database that matched DNA samples from the crime scene, they searched Ancestry.com's—where a close match did pop up. Investigators wanted to know more about the match, so they issued a court order to Ancestry.com requiring the company to share identifying information about the person. That individual was Michael Usry Sr.[65]

We're all vulnerable to governments potentially disrupting our lives due to some kind of data we've generated. Sometimes— as in Michael Usry Jr.'s case—the data doesn't even need to be ours.

To further complicate things, rules around what constitutes personal data and how it must be handled are different throughout the world. In the absence of federal regulations in the United States, laws vary from state to state and even from city to city. For example, there are restrictions about how law enforcement can use facial recognition technology in some US states and cities.[66] But as rules on biometrics are being written and rewritten, police have used it to detrimental effects. The *New York Times* reported that studies by MIT and the National Institute of Standards and Technology (NIST) have found that while the technology works relatively well on white men, the results are less accurate for other demographics.[67] NIST research noted that algorithms falsely identified African American and Asian faces ten to one hundred times more than Caucasian faces.[68]

That imperfect technology may have contributed to cases of mistaken identity of at least three Black men in reports we've found. In 2022, Randal Reid was arrested in Georgia after a facial recognition algorithm wrongly flagged him as a match with video footage capturing the theft of luxury goods in a Louisiana thrift store. Reid told police he had never been to Louisiana a day in his life. But he spent nearly a week in jail before authorities realized their mistake and set him free.[69] Reid's case was not unique. In 2020, Robert Julian-Borchak Williams was detained by Detroit police for thirty hours when facial recognition technology matched him for a theft crime that he did not commit.[70] And in 2019, Nijeer Parks sued police, the prosecutor, and the City of Woodbridge, New Jersey, after he spent ten days in jail and about $5,000 to defend himself because facial recognition technology led police to accuse Parks of shoplifting candy and trying to hit a police officer with a car.[71]

The United States needs better regulations that mandate the ways law enforcement can use our private data to prosecute us. Many government leaders are advocating for this, but while we wait for more robust protection, our privacy and well-being continue to be at risk.

The challenge, too, is that we likely wouldn't want to block law enforcement from using private data entirely. Good things have come from their work with it. There are countless reports of criminals having been caught and innocent people exonerated thanks to innovations in DNA research. Cell phone location data was crucial in helping Milwaukee police locate the two men responsible for the kidnapping and rape of a Minnesota health care worker in 2017, and it's provided useful evidence in numerous other crimes.[72] But all this progress has come at a cost. The US is not a surveillance state, although the more that things like our biometrics, private messages, exercise routines, Facebook friends, family lineage, and personal interests become fodder for government interference in our lives, the more our civil rights and liberties are potentially compromised.

We're not just concerned about freak misunderstandings that eventually work themselves out. Our lives are constantly changing, and we can never know how something we say, write, or do today will affect a future situation. You may find yourself in divorce court next year facing a custody battle for your children with your private texts and emails used as evidence against you. Or maybe you decide to attend a protest to support a cause that's important to you, and simply being in a certain place at a certain time with your cell phone gets you on law enforcement's radar as a crime suspect. Maybe you feel you have nothing to hide. But your data can tell a different story.

And, if all this seems a bit extreme, ask yourself this. Do you behave differently when your webcam is on? With your webcam on, you may be in smart clothes, talking to your coworkers in a conference call. But with your webcam off, you are maybe in sweatpants, playing with your kids or talking to your dog in a dog-parent voice. Would you want your boss to hear that? And that is why privacy matters. Because we all behave differently when we know we are being watched or monitored.

Where Have You Been?
That's Pretty Easy to Figure Out.

I want to turn the spotlight on location data because law enforcement has come to rely on it so much in recent years. But its popularity isn't the only reason it stands out. Location data is unique because it's a form of personal data that law enforcement frequently taps into but that they can only get from private companies. And *whether they should access it at all* is a hotly debated issue.

Now, to be clear, governments access a lot of personal data about us from sources that they own. The FBI has had a national DNA database since 1998,[73] for example, and some US cities like Detroit have police-run video surveillance systems that they've used in tandem with facial recognition software.[74] Officials get similar data from private companies, but they do have their own sources. Then, of course, there is the standard set of personal information the government has on all of us: our tax records, addresses, details about our family, race, gender . . . on and on.

Location data is a different animal—and so is its sometimes eyebrow-raising by-product, geofencing. Geofencing is a form of data collection that sets a virtual perimeter around a location and identifies when a mobile device is within that area. Investigators have found that location data generated by geofence reports can be helpful in identifying crime suspects—sometimes to a fault, as we've seen—but they rely on private companies for the information. Law enforcement has leaned on Google as a key source for geofence data over the last several years, although Google is far from their only option. There is an $18.52 billion data-broker industry dedicated to aggregating and selling location data.[75]

The Fourth Amendment requires investigators to have a search warrant before they can access location data, and those warrants have been plentiful. Google reported that they received over twenty-thousand geofence warrants from law enforcement between 2018 and 2020 ordering them to identify users based on their location history information.[76] Apple sees far fewer warrants (only thirteen in 2022), perhaps because, as they say in their 2022 transparency report, they don't have any data to provide in response to geofence requests.[77] Even if we remove those tech giants from the picture, there are always other private companies, including data brokers, that can provide location data.

The AP reported that a company called Fog Data Science, developed by two former high-ranking Department of Homeland Security officials, has sold location data to local police departments around the United States. Another company, Venntel, has sold location data to agencies including Immigration and Customs Enforcement (ICE) and the FBI. Plus, it seems that a warrant isn't always in place before the data is shared. AP's report notes that "the Department of Homeland Security's watchdog is auditing how the offices under its control have used commercial data. That comes after some Democratic lawmakers asked it to investigate US Customs and Border Protection's use of Venntel data to track people without a search warrant in 2020."[78]

Despite these concerns, it helps to remember that collecting location data isn't inherently bad. Much like cookies, we probably rely on the efficiency that our location data facilitates more than we realize. Google says location history helps it provide users with useful, meaningful experiences—from driving directions to making sure our search results include things near us.[79] We all get this. Many drivers don't remember a world where they didn't rely on their phone's navigation app to guide them to a new place. And we'd be pretty annoyed if we searched for "coffee near me" and got results for Austin, Texas, coffee shops when we were actually in Phoenix, Arizona.

Advertisers can leverage precise location data to serve hyper-targeted ads. We've seen some fun, creative ad campaigns come out of that feature. In 2018, Burger King created a marketing campaign that actually got people to walk out of McDonald's and go to the nearest Burger King instead. They called it the Whopper Detour, and it worked by sending a notification to someone's phone offering a one cent Whopper when they were within six hundred feet of a McDonald's restaurant. Folks could just tap the coupon, preorder their food through the BK app, and head to the nearest Burger King to pick it up. Burger King trolled McDonald's in an effort to drive downloads of their BK app, and it worked. The app was downloaded a million times within thirty-six hours of the campaign's launch.[80] It even hit the number one spot on Apple's App Store.[81]

The Whopper Detour's secret sauce was geofencing, and Burger King's virtual perimeter was a six-hundred-foot radius around McDonald's restaurants.

That "virtual perimeter" is what's so useful to law enforcement. Google has been able to tap into its location data archives to see who was within a specific radius at a specific time. Geofence data has helped solve many criminal investigations, but it also raises privacy concerns. Geofence searches contributed to Jorge Molina and Zachary McCoy getting on local police's radar for crimes they didn't commit. Its ongoing use in criminal investigations has privacy advocates, judges, and lawmakers divided on whether the practice is constitutional. In 2020, federal Illinois judge Gabriel A. Fuentes deemed a warrant unconstitutional when it was requested to assist in locating a suspect in the theft of prescription medication, stating in his court order, "Simply because Google can collect this information, or because the government can obtain it from Google under a 'constrained' approach 'justified' by the investigation's parameters, does not mean that the approach clears the hurdles of Fourth Amendment probable cause and particularity."[82]

Fuentes clarified that his ruling does not suggest geofence warrants are categorically unconstitutional but that they should be considered on a case-by-case basis. He also pointed out in his court order that "the potential to use Google's capabilities to identify a wrongdoer by identifying . . . nearly everyone . . . at the time and place of a crime may be tempting. But if the government can identify that wrongdoer only by sifting through the identities of unknown innocent persons without probable cause and in a manner that allows officials to 'rummage where they please in order to see what turns up,' even if they have reason to believe something will turn up, a federal court in the United States of America should not permit the intrusion. Nowhere in Fourth Amendment jurisprudence has the end been held to justify unconstitutional means."[83] Fuentes's words remind us of Warren and Brandeis's 1890 *Harvard Law Review* article, "The Right to Privacy." Again, not much has changed in a couple centuries. Tech innovations constantly spark new conversations and concerns about what is considered an invasion of privacy.

As judges approve or deny geofence warrants on a case-by-case basis, some leaders want to see them gone for good. In New York, the proposed Reverse Location and Reverse Keyword Search Prohibition Act would make New York the first state to ban these warrants.[84]

Corporate leaders are also taking action. One week after the Supreme Court overturned *Roe v. Wade* on June 24, 2022, Google SVP Jen Fitzpatrick announced that Google would delete entries from a person's location history if Google's system identified that they visited a location that could reveal personal information about them, including counseling centers, domestic violence shelters, abortion clinics, fertility centers, addiction treatment facilities, weight loss clinics, and cosmetic surgery clinics.[85] This was a welcome change as fears surged over how personal data might be used to criminalize people seeking or assisting with abortions after *Roe v. Wade* was overturned. It has already been widely reported that people's keyword searches, texts, private messages, and purchases have been used as evidence to convict people of abortion-related crimes.[86] Google's pledge to delete sensitive location data eases some worries as regulations remain a moving target.

Then, in December 2023, Google took its role as a data steward to the next level by announcing a change in how it saves location data. Moving forward, data will be saved on each device, not on the cloud, and if users opt to save their data on the cloud, it will be encrypted so no one can read it, including Google.[87] This means that in the future Google will no longer be able to provide location data in response to geofence warrants. That's encouraging from a consumer privacy standpoint, but it doesn't erase the problem when an entire industry of data brokers can still provide location data that they collect and aggregate via apps and other sources outside of Google.

Geofencing also raises privacy concerns beyond search warrants. A one cent burger coupon can seem harmless, but some folks may feel an ad campaign that knows where they are is intrusive to their privacy. Sometimes it is unquestionably so. In 2015, Boston-based ad agency Copley Advertising leveraged geofencing's capabilities by setting geofence areas around reproductive health centers—including Planned Parenthood clinics and hospitals and doctor's offices that perform abortions—and serving ads on behalf of anti-choice organizations to women who entered those locations. The ads included text such as "Pregnancy Help," "You Have Choices," and "You're Not Alone" that, if clicked, directed the person to information about abortion alternatives.[88] The ads were served to women in the US cities of Columbus, New York City, Pittsburgh, Richmond, and St. Louis, but the ad agency's home state of Massachusetts would not tolerate them. In 2017, Copley's owner, John F. Flynn, reached a settlement with the Massachusetts attorney general to resolve allegations that the ads would violate consumer protection laws in Massachusetts because they intrude upon a consumer's private health, medical affairs, or medical status and may result in gathering and disseminating private health facts about the consumer without their knowledge or consent.[89] While Copley Advertising seems to have since shut its doors, they're just one example of how geofencing has been used in unsettling ways.

Geofencing is here to stay, no matter how many concerns it may raise. Its market size in 2023 was $1.47 billion, and it's estimated to reach $4.19 billion by 2028.[90] And let's remember that geofencing is not inherently bad. It has many benign, practical applications—for example, in your privacy program, it can help you determine which cookie banner to serve based on privacy laws in a user's location (more on this in Part 2). But those aren't the functions of geolocation data that tend to get the spotlight or raise eyebrows.

What's the Price of Our Personal Data?

People who feel they lead boring lives with nothing to hide may still not be alarmed by all of this. But what many folks don't consider is that as cultural, societal, leadership, and governmental changes take place, new perspectives can change how our actions are viewed. Activities that were once considered harmless can be held against us and our fellow citizens. Information you previously shared about yourself or data you generated can even turn into admissions to crimes. Think about it: laws related to actions like medical procedures, uses of certain drugs, and who we can marry have changed worldwide in recent years alone. What if a future US Supreme Court decision takes away certain civil liberties that we value? It happened with abortion when *Roe v. Wade* was overturned in 2022. We don't know what future government leaders will stand for, how societal perspectives will change, or how our actions may be interpreted under evolving laws.

Our concerns also go beyond criminal accusations. The issue of governments' access to personal data through private companies is rife with problems. The situation is especially sticky in the United States, where the data broker industry is largely unregulated, and yet government agencies often rely on private brokers to carry out their work.

In just one example, it's been widely reported that ICE searched a database of personal information provided by LexisNexis over 1.2 million times between March and September 2021 alone.[91] And the *Intercept* reported that in 2021, LexisNexis entered a $16.8 million contract with ICE, wherein the data broker is providing ICE with access to billions of records containing personal data aggregated from public and private sources, including credit history, bankruptcy records, license plate images, and cellular subscriber information.[92]

LexisNexis faces ongoing backlash for the deal. In 2022, it was sued over its mass collection and sale of Illinoisans' data without their consent.[93] Antonio Gutierrez, strategic coordinator for Organized Communities Against Deportations (one of the advocacy groups behind the lawsuit), explained, "LexisNexis is violating individuals' privacy rights by providing addresses, phone numbers, relatives' names, and more through the data being sold to agencies like ICE without their permission."[94] Meanwhile, LexisNexis has been in the spotlight for reporting inaccurate data. Along with Experian, it was part of a 2022 class action lawsuit claiming that it published inaccurate and derogatory credit information, failed to maintain reasonable procedures in accurately reporting credit information, and failed to properly investigate credit information.[95] ICE is using its data nonetheless. And this is just one glimpse into the larger problem.

Many US lawmakers are trying to incite change. In August 2022, members of Congress sent a letter to the heads of several government agencies, including the FBI, the Department of Homeland Security, the Department of Justice, Customs and Border Protection, the Drug Enforcement Administration, and ICE, among others, urging them to disclose information about contracts they may have with data brokers.[96] And the Fourth Amendment Is Not for Sale Act, which aims to close government loopholes that allow law enforcement and intelligence agencies to purchase private data from data brokers, is making its way through Congress as of this writing.[97]

As legislation around government access to private data evolves and unfolds, our roles as data stewards become more important than ever. We must do our due diligence to be aware of all the third parties with whom we're sharing our users' data. And we need to be clear about how the third parties with whom we're sharing our data will use it. That can feel like a tall order, but the good news is that a strong data-privacy program will make these actions a part of your typical workflow. We have more power to protect personal data than it may seem.

TL;DR CHEAT SHEET

- The presence of data protection laws varies worldwide.
- There are no comprehensive federal data laws in the United States, and state laws vary heavily, giving the US government lots of leeway to rummage around in its citizens' private lives.
- Some governments can access personal information such as an individual's private messages, their photos, their phone location, and even data about their menstrual cycle, daily routines, dating profiles, and exercise patterns.
- In the US, the Fourth Amendment can be interpreted to allow authorities to access an individual's private data with a warrant and then use that data to prosecute them. Additionally, there are no laws forbidding the government from buying data about citizens from data brokers.

(continued...)

- Currently, the Fourth Amendment Is Not for Sale Act, which aims to prevent government agencies from purchasing private data from data brokers, is making its way through Congress.
- "I have nothing to hide" misses the point that data can be misleading and cause your life to be disrupted by getting shut out of your email or bank accounts, flagged for suspicious behavior, wrongly accused of crimes, or even prosecuted based on incomplete or inaccurate data. Citizens have already been arrested, spent time in jail, and incurred legal expenses in addition to experiencing psychological distress, losing jobs, dropping out of school, or suffering other material and mental pain as a result of data being accessed about them that was misleading or inaccurate.
- Private companies like Apple have adapted by encrypting user information to prevent law enforcement warrants for geofencing data. In December 2023, Google followed suit.

CHAPTER 4

What Is Personal Information, Anyway?

B y now you know more about data privacy than most people
you'll ever meet. But here's a funny thing about this world:
one of the most confusing parts of navigating it is simply understanding what personal data *actually is*.

The problem is that there isn't one straightforward answer.
There isn't a universal definition for personal data because personal
data is defined differently under different laws. And not only that,
but laws are constantly evolving even as new ones are adopted across
regions, countries, states, and industries. And typically, the definitions leave some flexibility; this is essential when technologies evolve
and new datasets allow for identification. Just trying to keep up with
the basics is like chasing a moving target. In fact, by the time this book
publishes, the definitions and standards surrounding personal data will
have changed somehow.

But in many ways, that's the work. Having a strong data-privacy program means putting in the effort to stay on top of shifting laws, definitions, and standards that affect how you operate. It's a lot like marketing. Great marketers don't just learn the practice once and keep doing the same thing. They understand that they need to be thoughtful and constantly evolve their practices with what's current. If a marketer trying to reach teens ignores TikTok, they're likely going to fail. Likewise, if a payment-processing company ignores new regulations for how credit card information needs to be stored, they might face trouble down the road. If you want to succeed, you can't stick your head in the sand and just keep doing what you're doing forever.

I won't attempt to give you an all-inclusive list of data-privacy terms in this book because it's just not possible. But I'll give you something more powerful: guidance about how to develop a big-picture strategy for your data-privacy program that will cover your bases compliance-wise and help you build trust with your customers. Your program can also be agile enough to evolve with changing laws and definitions. The data-privacy world may be confusing, but that doesn't mean you have to be confused all the time. You can have a straightforward privacy program that keeps you ahead of the curve.

Creating that sort of program starts with an understanding of the basics of what data privacy is. I'll cover that in this chapter, and then we'll keep putting one foot in front of the other by building on that knowledge in the chapters ahead.

Personal Data 101

Before we talk about the privacy regulations you need to navigate (that's Chapter 5), let's get to the heart of what personal data is. While the definition varies, we define it broadly at Osano to capture as much as possible. Here's our umbrella definition, which is based on the GDPR and includes analogous terms under other regulations:

Personal Data: Also referred to as personal information (PI), this is any information that identifies, relates to, describes, is reasonably capable of being associated with, or could reasonably be linked (directly or indirectly) with a particular consumer or household.

It's the obvious stuff like your name, email, physical address, and phone number, but it also includes digital data like your IP address, device number, web browsing history, account numbers, and passwords. That said, context matters.

Take the name Mary Smith. With no other information attached to the name, jurisdictions wouldn't consider it personal data for any legal reason. Many Mary Smiths exist in the world, and if there's only a name to go off of, there's no way to know which Mary Smith is in question. However, if Mary Smith has a street address and phone number attached to her name in a single location or file, most jurisdictions would call that personal data. As such, companies in possession of Mary's data are beholden to data-privacy regulations.

Bottom line: The more information you have on a person, especially when collected in a single place, the more "personal" the data becomes. If you're ever in doubt, treat it as personal information.

Our definition generally excludes publicly available information or information that has been properly de-identified. The latter is usually done with software that makes the data look like gobbledygook but that your software can still understand and use to answer questions about the data. However, you need to make sure that the data cannot be re-identified. If someone can simply push a button and see the actual data, it's not really de-identified. It's just obscured.

We'll get into how some of the major privacy laws and regulations define personal data in Chapter 5. For now, it helps to know that this broad view covers most of the variances out there.

Next-Level Basics:
PII and Sensitive Information

The differences between definitions related to personal data are often subtle. And that can be nerve-racking. The best you can do when navigating this world is shed light on one element at a time and try not to get overwhelmed by the big picture. Now that you have a basic understanding of personal data, our next step is to examine two key groups of personal data: **personally identifiable information (PII)** and **sensitive information**.

Understanding PII

This may sound like a riddle, but it's not: all PII is considered personal data, but not all personal data is considered PII.[98]

PII is often an industry-specific term and consists of any information about a person—including data that can trace or distinguish their identity—and any information that can be linked to them (like medical, financial, or employment data).[99] But personal data on its own doesn't always consist of all those identifiers.

When we talk about **distinguishing** a person's identity, that means identifying one individual from another using specific data (like the Mary Smith example). **Tracing** that individual means you're processing enough data to understand aspects of that person's status or activities. As such, personal information like name, email, phone number, Social Security number, etc. are considered PII.

From a zoomed-out perspective, the greatest difference between personal data and PII is that PII is often used to differentiate one person from another, while personal data includes any information related to a living individual, whether it distinguishes them from another individual or not. Again, think of Mary Smith. Mary's name is her personal data, but it isn't PII since there are many Mary Smiths out there. Still, depending on the data-privacy regulations your organization is beholden to—i.e., the GDPR or others like it—the definition of PII can vary.

We'll get into more detail about how several data-privacy laws interpret the phrase in Chapter 5.

Understanding Sensitive Information

As an overarching definition, "sensitive information"—also known as "sensitive data"—is personal data that most jurisdictions believe should be treated with a higher standard of care. To protect it, your company may have to apply greater security measures. And, depending on the law, it's possible you'll need different kinds of consent to collect it.

If your organization allows unauthorized access to a data subject's sensitive information, you face a greater risk of being penalized by data-protection authorities. Permitting excessive access to sensitive data leaves a data subject open to various forms of harm and/or discrimination based on, for example, their sexual orientation, religious beliefs, private health matters, and the like.

Like most terms, the way each data-privacy law interprets sensitive information varies. For that reason, check your jurisdiction's definitions before your organization collects personal information. Again, we'll get into this in more detail in Chapter 5.

Personal Data's Curious Offspring: Derived Data

Our quest to define personal data has its challenges from the start, and it gets more complicated when we bring in its sometimes-questionable byproduct: **derived data**. Simply put, derived data is data that's created from other data that already exists. We can generate it ourselves with data we have on hand. It's also common for brokers and other data analysts to aggregate data from multiple sources and then use it to arrive at further conclusions about people. Remember: figuring out who people are and what they're drawn to is a highly lucrative business, and the more specific the information about a person is, the more valuable it is.

So, for example, a data broker may see that someone from your computer's IP address subscribed to an online exercise program, purchased cross-trainers from Underarmour.com, and ordered protein powder from Amazon.com. Those three data points alone will likely tag your IP address as belonging to a potential customer for health and fitness products, even though you never explicitly shared that information with anyone. The broker likely has similar information about millions of people's buying habits and compiles marketing lists that they then sell to anyone who might want that information—advertisers, the government, or whoever is willing to pay.

Firms also generate derived data with their in-house data all the time. Nordstrom.com may see that you have a pair of pants and a blazer in your shopping cart and based on that, suggest shoes and belts to you, even if you never searched for those items. They were able to deduce that you were perhaps shopping for a full outfit with the data they already had about you.

This sounds harmless enough. Maybe you don't mind seeing the suggestions for workout gear or outfit add-ons. Perhaps you even welcome them. But derived data can get tricky, fast.

A key challenge is that derived data's possibilities are open-ended and infinite. The ways in which it's created and used are constantly evolving, especially with AI in the mix, and those developments raise more questions than answers. For example, most privacy regulations give data owners (known as "data subjects") the right to request that their data be deleted, corrected, or modified. Data subjects can also dictate with whom a company shares their data, among other things. We can do this through what's called a subject rights request (SRR), which we'll cover on page 82.

SRRs are relatively straightforward when it comes to personal data that we've agreed to share with a company or organization. But what about derived data about us? Who technically owns it, and how can we monitor whether it's used in a way that violates our privacy? What if derived data about us is incorrect? How far removed from the individual does the data need to be before it is no longer the right of the individual to delete, remove, redact, or correct it? What if a company discovers that derived data they've accessed is wrong and needs to be corrected? Do they have an obligation to correct it downstream? And what about data that's derived from derived data?

The questions surrounding derived data, like the possibilities, are endless.

One of the most infamous data scandals of our time, which involved Facebook and the political consulting group Cambridge Analytica, shows us how powerful derived data can be. The story made headlines in 2015 when it was discovered that Facebook had allowed Cambridge Analytica to access millions of Facebook users' profile data without those users' permission.[100] Cambridge Analytica harvested the data by prompting Facebook users to download an app to take a personality quiz that billed itself as "a research app used by psychologists."[101] Facebook reported that roughly 270,000 people downloaded the app, and in so doing, they gave their consent for the app developer to access data such as their city, pages they'd liked, and some limited information about those users' friends.[102] Ultimately, the personal information of up to eighty-seven million Facebook users may have been shared with Cambridge Analytica in this way.[103] And Facebook let it happen. In 2022, Facebook's parent company Meta agreed to pay $725 million to settle a class-action lawsuit claiming it improperly shared users' information with Cambridge Analytica.[104]

That data was shared before major privacy regulations went into effect. And while we can't say that the Facebook/Cambridge Analytica fiasco inspired groundbreaking regulations like GDPR since it was already in development, it certainly brought data-privacy concerns into the public spotlight. Today's regulations make it so that this sort of data sharing is less likely to happen as companies work to develop strong data-privacy programs.

But there's more to the story. As we peel back its layers, it offers a fascinating look at what's possible with derived data. That personality quiz made its rounds on Facebook in 2014, not long before Cambridge Analytica was hired by then-presidential candidates Ted Cruz and Donald Trump to help them target voters. The company's then-CEO, Alexander Nix, has denied allegations that Cambridge Analytica used Facebook data in its work.[105] Even if it didn't, Nix revealed at the 2016 Concordia Annual Summit that by having hundreds and hundreds of thousands of Americans undertake a personality survey (whether it was the Facebook survey or some other one), it allowed them to "form a model to predict the personality of every single adult in the United States of America."[106]

The model he's talking about is psychographic profiling, which is a personality profile derived from aggregated data about individuals. The firm analyzed data from its surveys and classified people's personalities into five types following the OCEAN model: Openness, Conscientiousness, Extroversion, Agreeableness, and Neuroticism.[107] Then they tailored content for each personality type. Nix explained that if you know the personality of the people you're targeting, you can nuance your messaging to resonate more effectively with those key audience groups.[108] For example, when strategizing marketing and communications in elections, messaging related to Second Amendment rights would vary greatly for one personality group over another. For a highly Neurotic and Conscientious audience, Nix said you'd need a message that's rational and fear based. So for this group, you might posit that owning a gun is like having an insurance policy in the event of a burglary. For a Closed and Agreeable audience, which would likely include people who care about tradition, habits, family, and community, it would be more effective to have your messaging highlight those values when targeting those potential voters.[109]

In his talk, Nix described big data—which in this case refers to derived data—as the aggregation of as many individual data points as you can possibly get your hands on, which is then synthesized into one database and used to create insight about your target audience.[110] That's right on point. Nix said Cambridge Analytica had four to five thousand data points on every adult in the United States, which they used to target communications to each individual based on their personality type.[111] We can't know exactly where they got their data from, but their reach was tremendous.

This story is a prime example of what's possible with derived data and how valuable it can be. The Trump and Cruz campaigns paid Cambridge Analytica millions for its influential work using derived data. But, money aside, Cambridge Analytica was confident it could predict the personality of every adult in the US with data from hundreds of thousands of people. There are more than 250 million adults in the US.[112] That's a gigantic leap. And this happened a decade ago. The power of derived data has only grown as data analysts and marketers find new ways to draw conclusions about people from the information they have.

We're no longer living in the Wild West of the early- and mid-2000s, when data was everywhere for the taking with limited regulations in place to stop folks from grabbing any information they could. But that doesn't mean you can't still get value from derived data. If you lean on data to help your company grow, you're probably already familiar with how valuable derived data can be for generating revenue. And the good news is that having a strong privacy program doesn't mean you have to stop using it. You just need to be more thoughtful than ever about compliance and minimizing privacy risks. We'll guide you through best practices in the chapters ahead. For now, as we cover the basics, it's important to recognize that derived data is a wild card in the privacy world that's nearly impossible to contain, and the unknowns are magnified with each step that the data moves away from its original source.

Let's Talk about Consent

A benefit of the Facebook/Cambridge Analytica debacle and others like it over the last decade is that they brought data-privacy rights into the public consciousness just as regulations were emerging. It was serendipitous timing because regulations finally gave the public a straightforward way to assert their rights over how their data is collected and handled.

One of the major ways in which privacy regulations protect consumers is by requiring businesses to obtain clear, explicit consent from a consumer before they collect and use their data. Every regulation requires consent in some form, which means consent management will be a major piece of any privacy program. I'll show you how to build the consent arm of your privacy program in Chapter 9. For now, it helps to have a general understanding of consent's role in the data-privacy landscape.

At a minimum, you'll want a robust consent-management framework to avoid legal trouble and fines. The EU's Data Protection Authorities can issue fines of up to $24.1 million (€20 million) or 4 percent of annual global turnover for GDPR noncompliance, whichever is higher. A business in violation of the California Privacy Rights Act (CPRA) is subject to fines of up to $2,500 for each incidental violation or $7,500 for each intentional violation.[113]

But arguably more important, a strong consent-management framework builds public trust. A report by McKinsey on consumer data and privacy has shown that even consumers who haven't been impacted by data breaches watch how companies respond to them. The report highlighted that 71 percent of respondents said they would stop doing business with a company if it gave away sensitive data without permission.[114] So however you look at it, a robust consent-management strategy is essential.

Consent management is your organization's way of informing users of how you collect and use data and gives them the opportunity to consent or refuse such use. This can be a process, system, policy, or set of policies; compliant consent management generally includes more than one best practice.

Your goal is to build a holistic approach that complies with the spectrum of data-privacy laws relevant to your organization. The big ones for most organizations are the GDPR and the CPRA. You'll capture many requirements under other regulations if you comply with those two regulations. The EU's ePrivacy Directive (a.k.a. the Cookie Law) also plays a big role in how organizations handle consent. We'll take a closer look at each of these in Chapter 5.

Given its reach, let's look at what's required under the GDPR. Before processing any personal data, a business must ask the data subject for explicit permission using precise language. These are the GDPR's strict rules for consent:

- Consent must be "freely given, specific, informed, and unambiguous." You can't coerce a data subject into giving consent, lie about the purpose of the consent, or hide the intent of data processing in hard-to-understand language.
- When you ask for consent, your communication must be "clearly distinguishable from the other matters" and presented in "clear and plain language." You can't bury

the language in another document, or, say, in the fine print
of a personality quiz.

- Data subjects can withdraw their consent whenever
  they want. It must be as easy to withdraw consent
  as it is to give it. You are obligated to honor their decision.
  If you process their data for another purpose, you must
  get their consent again.
- An organization cannot obtain continuous, blanket consent. A new request for consent is required each time data
  is used for a new purpose.
- Children under thirteen can only give consent if they have
  permission from their parents.
- You must keep documentation of their consent or refusal.

Separately, the EU's ePrivacy Directive requires businesses with websites in the EU or who do business with customers in the EU to inform
users about cookie use and give them an opportunity to refuse the files.
Websites that are operated solely in the United States or other countries not covered by the GDPR and don't do business in the states
that have passed privacy laws may include a statement warning users
that the site is intended only for residents of certain countries. Even
if a company is willing to ignore millions of potential customers, however, there is no guarantee that such a warning would be sufficient
to avoid possible penalties if the company knowingly collects information about users in EU countries or in states that do have data-privacy
laws, like California, Virginia, and Connecticut.

Types of Consent: Opt in, Opt out, or Hybrid

Figuring out the right approach to consent can be complicated, as rules vary under different laws. There are two main types: **opt out** and **opt in**. If your business has a website and you want to make it compliant with data-privacy laws, then identifying whether you need opt-in or opt-out consent is one of the first things you should do. Enforcement agencies tend to look at cookies first since they are a clear and simple way to determine whether a business is in compliance or not.

Opt-out consent means a company can do what they say in their privacy policy until a person "opts out" of that data use. With this option, a user must take an action, like unchecking a pre-checked box or filling out a form, to withdraw their consent for data to be collected and used. If they don't explicitly opt out, they are granting consent to most data-processing activities by default.

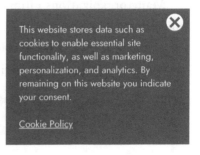

Opt-in consent means a company can't process a user's data (which includes collecting it in the first place) until that user takes an action to confirm their consent.

The GDPR requires consent to be opt in. So when a consumer visits an EU website for the first time, that business might ask for their consent in a cookie banner. If the consumer doesn't click "Accept" then the business can't drop cookies on the consumer's browser and, as a result, can't track their behavior. On the other hand, the CPRA and other state privacy laws only stipulate that consumers have

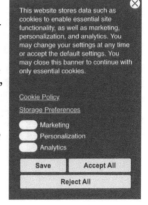

the right to opt out. The California Department of Justice defines the right to opt out as "the right to tell a business to stop selling their personal information."[115] Since opt-in consent is not explicitly required for non-sensitive personal information, opt out is usually the default consent model among US companies. Businesses under an opt-out law might present a banner with no accept or reject button whatsoever and notify the consumer that by continuing to use the website, they are consenting to cookies. Of course, some laws require cookie banners to provide opt-out options or, as is the case with the CPRA, links on the homepage that allow consumers to opt out.

Many organizations ultimately use a hybrid consent model, which incorporates elements of both opt in and opt out depending on the type of data being collected and how that data is being used. An example of a hybrid model would be a company using an opt-out method unless it's collecting sensitive personal information. In that instance, the company would switch to opt in and receive a user's explicit consent to collect and process personal data. A hybrid model can provide companies with a solution to be legally compliant with GDPR, CPRA, and other standards while giving users control of their data privacy—a win-win.

Opt In	Opt Out
Opt-in consent requires users to take a specific action that gives a business consent to collect and use their information. These activities include ticking a box, clicking a button, or taking another proactive measure to establish consent. Businesses may utilize these opt-in methods for newsletters, subscriptions, and cookies, or other data trackers.	The opt-out model requires businesses to divulge that they collect and use information and gives consumers the option to opt out. In contrast to the opt-in model, companies using the opt-out model assume consent until a person takes action to revoke permission.

Reclaiming Our Data

OK, so you've done your due diligence and locked in consent before collecting anyone's data. You're doing great. But the work doesn't stop there. Under most major privacy legislation, data subjects still have rights over that data, and they're empowered to exercise those rights at any time. We'll take a closer look at the full list of data-subject rights in the next chapter. For now, an important initial step is to know that a key way people can assert those rights is through subject rights requests (SRRs). SRRs allow a data subject to learn what an organization knows about them and how the organization uses that information. They also let people delete their data, modify it, dictate with whom companies share it, and more.

Let's start exploring SRRs by breaking down the name. The term "data subject" simply refers to the person whom data is about. Think of it this way: If you collect someone's data, that doesn't mean you own it. The data subject just gave you permission to collect and use it, either by explicitly clicking "I Agree" on a cookie banner or by continuing to use your website or application after being presented with a data-privacy disclosure. Since that personal information belongs to the data subject, they can dictate how you use it. When they make a request in that regard, it's an SRR.

As we navigate the basics of personal data, SRRs are a core part of the big picture. Research shows that 94 percent of consumers want more control over the data they share with companies and more insight into how that data is used. What's more, 77 percent of consumers say they factor transparent data practices into their purchasing decisions, with 30 percent *only* buying products that have demonstrated transparency.[116] SRRs play a big role in offering that transparency.

SRRs are a great solution to addressing consumer demand for control over their data, but they're not available to everyone. Companies are only required to fulfill those privacy rights requests when a data subject is in an area that is protected by a privacy law. In other words, someone in Florida might not have the ability to request what data, say, their mortgage company collected about them. Or, even if they asked, the company may not be legally required to respond because Florida's data-privacy law (the Florida Digital Bill of Rights, or FDBR) only applies to businesses that earn more than $1 billion in revenue, and there is no federal data-privacy law that would preempt the FDBR (at least, not at the time of this writing). But someone in California who is a customer of that same mortgage company can make the request, and the company would be legally obligated to answer them under requirements of the CPRA— assuming the company meets the CPRA's thresholds.

That said, just because it's not required doesn't mean you can't do it. Companies may choose to fulfill data-subject rights requests beyond compliance requirements for a number of reasons, including the following:

- They consider it the right thing to do.
- It builds a better business and customer experience.
- They want to support equal privacy rights.

As you evaluate the path that's best for your business, it helps to balance your core values with operational demand. If opening SRRs to everyone, even if it's not required, means you may be fulfilling ten extra requests annually, doing so may be worth the benefits. But if it potentially means you're fulfilling ten thousand additional requests, that's a bigger decision that may involve more resources.

The 411 on SRRs

Each data-privacy regulation has its own set of data-subject rights as well as rules and procedures surrounding SRRs. Again, we'll take a closer look at these in Chapter 5. Let's focus on the basics for now.

A person can submit an SRR to an organization and, upon receipt, the organization must provide the respective information or take certain requested actions. Essentially, when your business receives an SRR from a data subject, you need to take the appropriate action with any information you have on the subject.

SRRs aren't new; organizations and governments have accepted them from consumers for years, originally as data access requests. But recent consumer data-privacy regulations introduced several changes that made it easier for individuals to make additional requests. The changes go a long way toward transparency in data processing, but they can create challenges for companies and organizations.

Individuals don't need a reason to submit an SRR. In response to a request, the only questions an entity may ask are those that verify a subject's identity and help locate the requested information. Admittedly, this can be a burden—especially if you don't keep all of a subject's data in one convenient place. In the chapters ahead, we'll guide you on how to implement a data-mapping process to keep track of data and where it's kept and give you suggestions for reporting tools you can use to cull information from multiple sources.

What You Need to Include in an SRR Response

Your response will depend on the data subject's request. Let's look at some of the most common types of requests.

Data summary SRRs: When responding to a data summary SRR, your organization would typically provide a complete list of all personal information you have on a subject. In some cases, the subject may request only specific details. You are obligated to provide whatever information the subject requests. Always remember that different laws grant different rights, so make sure to review your relevant law to see what you need to provide.

Deletion SRRs: Consumers can also request that you delete all the data you have on them, commonly referred to as **the right to erasure or the right to be forgotten.** A data subject might also request that you delete only certain types of data. Usually, they'll have requested a data summary first. If they see something in the summary that they aren't comfortable with your organization storing, they might ask you to delete just that specific data from your systems.

SRRs for correction: Sometimes data subjects don't mind that you have collected their personal information, but they've noticed an error in the data or their personal information has changed. In this case, they might make an SRR to ask you to correct the erroneous information.

SRRs to opt out of the sale or share of personal information: Under certain data-privacy regulations, consumers can ask that you stop any transfers of their personal information to third parties. Your exact requirements can differ depending upon the regulation at play.

Who Can Submit an SRR?

Most data-privacy laws allow any consumer to submit an SRR. Some laws exclude employees, commercial partners, job candidates, and the like from submitting SRRs, but that's not the case with some of the largest jurisdictions covered by data-privacy laws. An individual can sometimes submit an SRR on behalf of another person, such as in the case of a parent or guardian, a court-appointed official handling someone's affairs, or a data subject simply asking for help from a friend or relative. In these instances, it's your organization's responsibility to ensure the request is genuinely on behalf of the data subject. In response to this SRR type, you're allowed to ask for supporting evidence of the relationship, like a birth certificate that names parents, guardianship paperwork, or power of attorney documentation.

Not as many of the modern, comprehensive privacy laws include employees as data subjects, but as of this writing, California and the EU currently permit employees to submit SRRs, with similar rights coming into effect in some newer state laws such as those in Oregon and Delaware. When an employee submits an SRR, you need to pay special attention to the request. For one, your business will likely collect more personal information and more sensitive personal information from your employees. Under certain laws, sensitive personal information (like Social Security numbers, ethnicity, sexual orientation, and driver's license numbers) carries higher penalties for any associated violations. Furthermore, employee SRRs are more likely to be triggered by a perceived wrong. A consumer might make an SRR out of curiosity; an employee might do so to see why they were passed over for promotion or why they've been put on a performance improvement plan. Lastly, most data-privacy laws prohibit businesses from retaliating against somebody for making an SRR. If an employee makes an SRR and their role is later terminated, they might file a complaint with the attorney general or try to sue—even if the two events were unrelated.

The bottom line on SRRs is that they're a key vehicle in allowing data subjects to exercise their rights. It's important to understand them, anticipate them, and be ready to respond to them *well*. That means on time, in full, and in an organized manner. How an organization handles SRRs is a key indicator of how much that organization prioritizes data subjects' privacy and, in turn, how much data subjects can trust that company with their personal information. The good news is that a strong data-privacy program will make it much easier to reply to SRRs and earn that trust. An underdeveloped privacy program will have you scrambling to pull together every SRR response and put you at risk of noncompliance and broken trust. By the time you're done reading this book, you'll know what to do to be in that first group.

What Now, What Next?

It's hard knowing what to do in a world where the questions are as abundant as the answers. Definitions of personal data change from one law to the next. New data is created from old data that takes on a life of its own. And as organizations try to simply understand what data they're collecting and how they may need to handle it, they're responsible for delivering that information back to data subjects any time a request lands in their lap.

It's a lot for individuals and organizations to juggle, and the factors involved are only growing. We all put more personal data into the world every single day. Every purchase, every internet search, every form we fill out, every post or interaction we make with a social media site is another crumb we add to our personal data trail. As we've seen, our personal data can be accessed without any action on our part. Conclusions can be made about our political preferences, our life events, our health, or any other aspect of our lives.

And we have to wonder: What will having all of this available data about us mean over the years as it continues to accumulate? What will it mean for our kids, some of whom have had their entire lives documented online—from information their parents shared since their birth to what they later share about themselves? Will it only give others more power to influence us, as custom content is delivered to us one by one? This has already been going on in marketing for years. But our personal information is used to influence us in more ways than we may think.

There are many known instances of what disinformation expert Nina Jankowicz calls "foreign disinformation actors" participating in controversial conversations within US communities, seemingly for the purpose of stirring societal discord. In 2021, it was discovered that social media accounts based in Kazakhstan were participating in conversations about the Austin, Texas, Independent School District's decision to mandate masks in response to the COVID-19 pandemic. In fact, accounts based in Kazakhstan were the second-most active when it came to posting comments on the topic on the Austin Independent School District's social media pages, behind only US-based profiles.[117] And this was not an isolated incident. In 2016, both anti-Islam and pro-Islam Facebook and Instagram groups created by Russian actors organized live protests in the streets of Houston, Texas, to rouse turmoil within American communities.[118] The *New York Times* has reported that social media bot accounts with ties to Russia regularly focus on spreading disinformation about topics that are divisive for Americans, like gun control or whether NFL players should kneel during the national anthem.[119]

This takes targeted content to a whole new level. It's one thing to get served an ad for shoes you may like. But when our personal information is used to pit us against one another, our collective peace is at risk. When communities are at odds with themselves, it causes people to lose trust in institutions, and it sparks conflicts such as election fraud claims.

Much of this is out of our hands, but like a lot of what I've covered in this book so far, awareness is our first step to empowerment. Many people think data privacy is about clicking "OK" on a website's cookie banner, but there is more to it than that. A strong data-privacy program isn't just about compliance. Individuals and communities depend on organizations to practice safe data handling to protect our privacy on so many levels.

Now that you understand the basics of what data privacy is and how society has reached a point of needing regulations to keep our data safe, let's look at the major privacy laws that are likely to inform your privacy program.

TL;DR CHEAT SHEET

- There is no universal definition of what personal data or personal information (PI) is because it's defined differently under different laws and in different industries, states, and countries.
- Osano follows the GDPR guidelines and defines PI as anything that identifies, relates to, describes, associates with, or is linked to a particular consumer or household. In other words, names, emails, SSNs, physical addresses, phone numbers, but also IP addresses, device numbers, web browsing history, account numbers, and passwords are all considered PI.
- Personally identifiable information (PII) is an industry term for data you can use to trace or distinguish someone's identity. All PII is PI, but not all PI is PII.
- The name Mary Smith is PI but not PII because there are many individuals of that name. Together with a phone number or address it becomes PII because you can now distinguish an individual.
- Sensitive data or sensitive information (SI) is PI that should be handled with higher standards of privacy, such as information about one's sexual orientation, religious beliefs, or private health matters that may expose an individual to harm or discrimination. Companies are often more harshly penalized for not managing SI properly.

- Derived data is created from existing data. These are indirect conclusions that can be drawn about an individual based on the direct information that has already been collected. For example, a data broker may classify someone as interested in health and fitness because they bought activewear and have a gym membership.

CHAPTER 5

Data-Privacy Laws, and What They Mean for You

E verything we've covered so far brings us to the catalyst for building a formal data-privacy program: regulations. They're here, they're multiplying, and compliance requirements for most organizations are growing every year. As a last step before we dig into building your privacy program, let's take a broad look at the laws you'll likely orient your program around.

You're not alone if the thought of navigating data-privacy laws makes you want to bury your head in the sand. The past decade has thrown so much new legislation our way that we'd never had to deal with before; it can be overwhelming just figuring out where to start. It all began when the European Union's game-changing legal framework known as the General Data Protection Regulation (GDPR) went into effect in 2018, forever changing how the world treats

EU citizens' data. From then on, the floodgates were opened. Today, more than 130 countries have data-privacy legislation in place.[120] While a US federal data-privacy law is still up in the air, the California Privacy Rights Act (CPRA) gives data-protection rights to a huge number of US citizens—not to mention the alphabet soup of other US privacy laws in effect and the many more in the works.

Since the GDPR led the way, it's been a model for most other data-privacy laws that followed. That's good news because it means that once you have a strong understanding of the GDPR, you'll be familiar with the core concepts upon which most other privacy laws are built. The less-good news is that the GDPR is extremely dense. It's over 260 pages; more than fifty thousand words; and chock full of words like "pseudonymization," "dactyloscopic data," and "derogation." In other words, it's not exactly a light beach read. However, you need to understand the GDPR and any other data-privacy laws that apply to your organization if you want to stay compliant.

That said, we want to get you beyond compliance. Compliance is just the status quo. It keeps the fines away, but it doesn't give you a competitive edge. Once you can confidently navigate the legislation that affects how you do business, it opens a world of opportunity to build trust with anyone who interacts with your brand, whether that's employees, vendors, or customers.

The first step is to get familiar with current laws and how they might affect your operations. That's what we'll cover in this chapter, starting with the big picture and drilling down to specific laws that apply to most organizations. This task isn't as overwhelming as it may seem precisely because the GDPR has informed so much of the data-privacy landscape. While it's a huge piece of legislation to process, you'll be well on your way to understanding the remaining laws that you need to pay attention to once you have a solid grasp on the GDPR.

Even better news is that the GDPR starts out with a rundown

of the seven principles that are at the heart of the law. So while we still need to dig into the details of the law, it's a huge help to know the GDPR's core purpose up front. Here are those seven principles:

1. **Lawfulness, fairness, and transparency:** Processing data should abide by the law, treat data subjects fairly, and be transparent.

2. **Purpose limitation:** Companies should only process data for legitimate purposes that they specify for each data subject before they collect it.

3. **Data minimization:** Data processors must collect and use only the data absolutely necessary to complete their business and limit access to personal data to only those employees needing the information to complete the process consented to by the data subject.

4. **Accuracy:** Organizations should keep their data accurate at all times.

5. **Storage limitation:** Organizations should only store personal data as long as necessary for the intended purpose. Organizations should delete the data when they're done with it.

6. **Integrity and confidentiality:** Organizations should process data to protect its security, integrity, and privacy. (For instance, transferring data with encryption.)

7. **Accountability:** Organizations are responsible for demonstrating GDPR compliance. Regulators expect detailed documentation about the data collected, how it's used, and where it's stored. Organizations must train staff well to implement organizational security measures. And organizations must have data-processing agreements in place with all third-party vendors who process data on their behalf.[121]

As you start getting familiar with the various data-privacy laws out there, you'll notice that they all aim to bring some sort of order to the way organizations collect, use, and handle personal data based on these principles. Most follow a notice and consent model—which means their rules revolve around how organizations notify data subjects of their personal data practices and how data subjects give consent to use their personal data. Those are the core similarities. Regulations vary a lot, which we'll help you navigate.

Privacy Legislation Terms and Concepts You Must Understand

You'll have an easier time understanding privacy laws if you're familiar with the key terms most of them use. Here are some of the most important ones.

- **Personal Data or Personal Information:** Any information that can directly or indirectly identify an individual. This includes names, email addresses, ethnicity, zip codes or other location information, gender, banking details, IP addresses, biometric data, religious and political beliefs, web cookies, and even social media posts. Jump to Chapter 4 for a deeper dive into personal data definitions.
- **Data Processing:** Any action performed on data, including manual and automatic methods.
- **Data Controllers:** The people who decide why, when, and how personal data is processed.
- **Data Subject:** A person whose data is processed. Think customers, subscribers, and the like.

- **Data Processor:** Any third-party organization that engages in processing personal data, including email marketing tools, analytics tools, and cloud vendors.
- **Accountability:** Technical and organizational measures put in place by organizations to demonstrate what they did with data and why it was necessary.
- **Transparency:** Clear communication by organizations to data subjects about data processing in a way that's "easily accessible and easy to understand" and uses "clear and plain language."
- **Privacy by Design:** Data protection through technology design.

Europe Led the Way

A little history helps us understand why we are where we are. Europe has always been ahead of the game on data protection. As we covered earlier, the world's first data-protection law was enacted in Germany in 1970. Since then, the European Union has led the rest of the world in data protection and online privacy legislation. The first comprehensive data-protection regulation, the EU Directive on Data Protection, was passed in the European Union in 1995, and it covered the collection, use, transfer, and security of personal information of residents of any European Union country. Then, in 2002, the EU passed the ePrivacy Directive, which requires each EU member state to pass its own national laws on data protection and privacy.[122] The ePrivacy Directive was amended in 2009 and regulates several important issues, such as consent, confidentiality, spam, cookies, and treatment of traffic data.

By 2012, the European Parliament realized that the Directive wasn't enough. Websites were vacuuming up user data at an unprecedented rate, and the existing hodgepodge of privacy laws across the member states was confusing and insufficient. That's when they decided to draft the GDPR. It went into effect in 2018, and it established core principles to govern the collection of personal information, along with strict penalties for violations of those principles. In combination with the ePrivacy Directive, the GDPR classifies any data created by an identifiable person as personal data and requires consent before collection of that data, along with granting people a number of rights to access, delete, correct, and object to the collection of their personal data.

The GDPR ushered in a wave of privacy legislation around the globe. As other countries sought to continue doing business with the European Union, and as our lives became more digital, protecting personal and sensitive data became a priority across regions and industries.

The EU continues to work diligently to advocate for optimal data handling. In 2020, the European Commission published a data strategy that outlines its vision of becoming a leading role model for a society empowered by data to make better decisions. The GDPR was a major step toward fulfilling that vision. Moving forward, the Commission's goal is to "create an attractive policy environment so that, by 2030, the EU's share of the data economy—data stored, processed and put to valuable use in Europe—at least corresponds to its economic weight, not by fiat but by choice." This vision takes data privacy to a whole new level, with an aim to create a single European market for data where businesses have easy access to a massive amount of high-quality industrial data without compromising individuals' rights.[123] We can be sure to see new legislation over the next decade as the EU continues implementing its data strategy.

Regulations vs. Directives

Data-privacy laws include many terms that don't usually come up in conversation. Two more important ones to understand and distinguish between are **directive** and **regulation**. What's the difference?

A **directive** is a flexible legislative instrument. It's an objective that EU member states must meet. States can implement a directive however they like as long as they achieve the desired result. They can adapt their existing laws or pass new ones.

A **regulation**, however, is more powerful than a directive. Once passed, a regulation is binding across all EU member states. It becomes enforceable on its set date. It does not need to be transposed into law at the state level, as it supersedes existing state law.

The GDPR, for example, is a regulation that replaced a directive (the Directive on Data Protection).

Why change from a directive to a regulation? Because state laws are all different. A single regulation makes things simpler for everyone to do business with each other.

Digging Into the GDPR

When the GDPR went live in 2018, it left many leaders outside the EU scratching their heads, wondering, "If the latest iteration of data privacy in the EU is meant to protect *them*, what does that have to do with *us*?" A lot, as it turned out. Although the GDPR is an EU-based law, it has what's called extraterritorial reach. This means that any organization with users, data subjects, or clients residing in the EU became subject to the GDPR's stricter data-privacy laws, especially as they pertained to cookie consent requirements and cookie consent record-keeping. It doesn't matter where the organization is based.

Make no mistake: Companies must comply with the GDPR or face hefty penalties—including fines and data-processing bans—if they offer goods or services to EU data subjects. Companies' partners are also on the hook. If you process data on behalf of a company that interacts with EU citizens, you must comply with the GDPR.

It can be hard for organizations to navigate their obligations under the GDPR or any other privacy laws that may apply to them. How do you even know which regulations you need to pay attention to? We'll help you figure that out.

Let's start with the big picture and zoom in as we go. We'll do that by taking a closer look at two big things that the GDPR regulates: how organizations **process personal information** and **data subjects' rights** over use of their personal data.

GDPR Requirements for Processing Personal Data

GDPR requirements govern almost every data point an organization collects across every conceivable online platform, especially if it's used to uniquely identify a person. Under the GDPR, organizations can only collect, store, process, or sell data if they can justify it with one of the following lawful bases:

1. **Consent:** The data subject gave specific consent to process the data. (Example: The subject gave you their email address to opt in to your email marketing list.) Consent plays a huge role in data-privacy compliance for the GDPR and beyond, so we'll cover it in more detail later in this chapter.

2. **Contract:** The processing is necessary to execute or prepare to enter into a contract with the data subject. (Example: You need to check their credit before approving a loan.)

3. **Legal Obligation:** You need to fulfill a legal obligation. (Example: You must process their data to comply with a court order.)

4. **Vital Interests:** The processing is necessary to protect the vital interests of the data subject or someone else. (Example: If you had to call for an ambulance to help a coworker in medical distress, you might tell the 911 dispatcher the person's full name and that he has a heart condition if that information is known to you and it is necessary to get your coworker proper medical care.)

5. **Public Task:** The processing is necessary to carry out a task of public interest.

6. **Legitimate Interest:** You're using the data in a way the data subject would expect given the service or product you're offering.

The United Kingdom's Information Commissioner's Office (ICO) points out that no single basis is "better" or more important than the others (though the data subject's consent is often the simplest and strongest legal basis to secure, so long as your internal compliance operations are in working order). Your basis will depend on your purpose and relationship with the individual.[124] The ICO also advises organizations to include their lawful basis and their purpose for processing data in their privacy notice and to take care to get it right the first time. Do not swap to a different lawful basis at a later date without good reason. In particular, you cannot usually swap from consent to a different basis.[125]

Data Subjects' Rights under the GDPR

In Chapter 4, we touched on the fact that data subjects have a set of rights under the GDPR. The goal in establishing these rights is to increase transparency and give data subjects control over their data and how it's used. When a data subject submits an SRR, they're exercising their rights to access and control the data that a company has on them. It's essential to know what those rights are so you can comply. They are:

The right to be informed that you've collected and used personal data. If you collected it from the subject yourself, you have to notify the data subject at the time of collection. Suppose you're a third-party vendor, for example, and obtained the data secondarily. In that case, the data subject must be informed within a "reasonable period of time," no later than thirty days, and in an easily accessible form.

The right to access personal data and how it's processed. A data subject can ask for a copy of all the data being processed about them. It's essential to have a mechanism to intake SRRs because a data subject can request a copy of the data, an overview of the categories of data you're processing, an explanation of why you're doing so, and a list of any parties with whom you're sharing the data.

The right to rectify inaccurate or incomplete personal data.
If an individual requests rectification (verbally or in writing), you have
one month to comply.

The right to erase data. Under this rule, a data subject has the right
to request that you erase their personal data within thirty days. Certain
conditions must exist for the request to be legitimate, of course. These
include situations when the data is no longer relevant, the original
purpose for collection has been satisfied, or a data subject withdraws
consent. If any of those apply, you have to stop processing and disseminating the subject's data.

The right to restrict the processing of personal data. If a data
subject requests this, you have to stop processing their data,
but you can still store it. Requests can be made verbally or in writing,
and you have thirty days to respond.

The right to data portability. Data subjects must be allowed
to take their data from one platform to another and do so easily,
safely, and securely. Data controllers must allow it without disrupting
its usability. You must provide data subjects with the entirety of their
data in a standard, machine-readable format.

The right to object. Data subjects can object to how their information is used for marketing, sales, or non-service-related purposes.
An organization must inform individuals of their right to object within
the first communication. Organizations must examine each objection,
but they can refuse to validate the objection if one of the following
is true:

- Legal or official authority is being carried out.
- The organization has a "legitimate interest" to process data
  to provide a data subject with a service they signed up for.
- A task is being carried out for public benefit.

The right to opt out of automated decision-making and profiling. Data subjects have the right to say no to solely automated decisions—including profiling—being made about their data that could have a legal or similarly significant effect on them. For instance, a website that automatically approves or denies people loans or makes hiring decisions would have a "significant effect" on their lives. Data subjects can opt out of these practices.

Organizations can refuse to respond to an SRR if the request is "excessive" or "manifestly unfounded," but you must be able to demonstrate why you consider a request to be manifestly unfounded or excessive. The ICO advises that to determine whether a request is manifestly excessive, consider whether it is clearly unreasonable. You can base this on whether the request is proportionate when balanced with the burden or costs involved in dealing with the request.[126]

Data Protection Officers

We can't unpack the GDPR without mentioning data-protection officers (DPO). The GDPR requires some organizations to designate a DPO to oversee the application of the GDPR and to protect personal data from misuse, unauthorized access, and other security breaches. You must appoint a DPO if:

1. You are a public authority (other than a court) acting in a judicial capacity.
2. Your core activities require you to monitor people on a large scale (e.g., Facebook's entire model revolves around tracking its users).
3. Your core activities include the processing of special categories of data listed under Article 9 or Article 10. You can find the full GDPR text at osano.com/gdpr-full-text.

That said, it's smart to appoint a DPO even if you aren't required to. It's good to have someone on staff who understands the GDPR and how it applies to your organization so that they can advise people in your organization about their responsibilities, monitor GDPR compliance, and work with supervisory authorities in the event of a data breach or other issue. If you're an organization based outside the EU, you must also appoint an EU-based person as a representative and point of contact for your organization's GDPR obligations.[127]

Simply knowing the GDPR requirements we've covered so far is a big step in understanding an organization's obligations under the law. There's more to the GDPR, of course. But before we take a closer look at GDPR specifics, let's look at other key data-privacy regulations that many organizations need to have on their radar. Because while the GDPR did inspire most of these, there are many differences among them. When you build your data-privacy program, you'll ideally do it in such a way that all of your obligations under every rule and directive that applies to you are satisfied. That may seem impossible, and the truth is, how attainable that goal is depends on your business's size, reach, industry, and complexity. But you need to try. We advise working with your legal counsel to guide you on what laws are applicable where you do business. In the meantime, let's look at what laws beyond the GDPR you may be obligated to comply with.

A Swirling World of Privacy Regulations

The world of privacy regulations gets complicated fast once we look beyond the GDPR. A core challenge is a lack of consistency across regions and industries. And it's not just that regulations vary from one area to the next. It's that three of the world's biggest regions— the European Union, the United States, and China—each have fundamentally different philosophies about data privacy. Experts

have referred to this dilemma as the tripolar privacy model.[128]
The EU is known to have an approach centered on the individual,
prioritizing the protection of user data above all else, as we've seen
in the GDPR. China's regulations emphasize maintaining the government's control over its citizen's data. Although its privacy law,
the Personal Information Protection Law (PIPL), shares lots
of similarities with the GDPR, a key difference is that it's enforced
by China's government rather than an independent third party.
The United States' data-privacy landscape has been shaped
by a longtime lack of federal regulations, leading some experts
to classify the country's philosophy as consumer-centric. A study
out of the University of Brazil referred to the United States' data-
privacy approach as an "innovation-first approach that does not take
matters such as privacy into great consideration."[129] In other words,
lacking a universal law to protect US citizens' data-privacy rights,
the major tech companies that benefit from the data have been free
to make up the rules as they go.

Despite numerous proposals over the years, no one comprehensive federal law governs data privacy in the US as of this writing. This
doesn't mean the US is totally lawless when it comes to data privacy.
It actually has a breadth of sectoral data privacy and data-security laws.
The US is also experiencing a massive drive toward pushing privacy
legislation at the state level. Rather than wait for the federal government to find a consensus on how to legislate broadly, state lawmakers
have been nudged by consumers, consumer advocates, and even companies to set their own rules.

The next few pages offer a bird's-eye view of key privacy laws
beyond the GDPR. This list, by nature, can't be exhaustive since
every organization has its unique circumstances, but if you're building a privacy program, it is a useful primer for navigating laws that
may be relevant to you.

California Privacy Rights Act

The most comprehensive and influential US state data-privacy legislation to date is the California Privacy Rights Act (CPRA). It came to be after a concerned citizen, San Francisco real estate developer Alastair Mactaggart, had an illuminating conversation with friends over pizza and wine at his home one night. The *New York Times* reported that Mactaggart asked his friend, a Google software engineer, whether he should be concerned about everything Google knew about him. The friend's response shocked him. "If people really knew what we had on them, they would flip out," he said.[130] These were pre-GDPR days, although the regulation was looming. The conversation led Mactaggart on a quest to incite change. He founded the privacy advocacy group Californians for Consumer Privacy (CCP) and put forth a proposition that led to the landmark 2018 California Consumer Privacy Act (CCPA). Not satisfied with where the CCPA eventually landed, the CCP pushed for another ballot measure in 2020, Proposition 24, which led to the CPRA. It superseded and replaced CCPA and went into effect in January 2023.

The CPRA is essentially the CCPA 2.0, and it covers the entirety of what you need to understand the California privacy law. It applies if you are a for-profit organization that "does business" in the state of California, collects the personal data of Californians or has it collected for you, and fits one or more of these criteria:

- Buys, sells, or shares the personal information of one hundred thousand people or households.
- Creates 50 percent or more of your revenue through the sale or sharing of personal information.
- Had $25 million in gross revenue in the preceding calendar year.

To stay in compliance with the CPRA, first, and most importantly, you need to make sure "consumers" (which includes your employees if they are California residents) can exercise their rights to control the collection and use of their personal data.

"Personal data" or "personal information" is defined in the CPRA as "information that identifies, relates to, describes, is capable of being associated with, or could reasonably be linked, directly or indirectly, with a particular consumer or household."[131] Unless you take steps to de-identify data after you collect it, much of the data you collect from customers and employees is personal data according to California law.

The CPRA puts the onus on organizations to make sure consumers (and employees) know their privacy rights, which means explaining their rights at the point of collection as part of the notice provided to people when they're giving you their data. Here is a rundown of those rights:

- **Right to Access, Deletion, and Correction:** Consumers must be able to obtain and delete their own personal information at any time and have it corrected if it is incorrect. If they ask you to delete it, you have to make anyone you've shared it with or sold it to delete it as well. As part of sharing their personal data with them, and in addition to the actual data you possess, you must provide consumers with a list of:

    »Categories of personal information you have collected.
    »Categories of sources from which you collected their personal information.
    »The business purpose for which you collected their data.
    »Categories of third parties to which you sell or share their data.

- **Right to Object to Sale or Share:** Consumers can prevent the sale or sharing of their information (and you need a "do not share" button on your website to make this easy).

- **Right to Opt Out of Behavioral Profiling and Automated Decision-Making:** Consumers can ask you to stop profiling and serving ads based on behavior, and they can ask you not to use automated decision-making to provide them with offers, products, services, etc.

- **Right to Object to the Use of Sensitive Personal Information:** For certain data, including data about race, precise geolocation, religion, union membership, genetics, biometrics, sexual orientation, and the contents of communications, consumers can stop you from using that data at all. This consumer right also requires you to have a prominent button or link people can use to "limit the use of my sensitive personal information."

- **Right to Data Portability:** If asked, you must transfer any personal data you hold about a person to another organization, "to the extent technically feasible, in a structured, commonly used, machine-readable format."

The CPRA also lays out the need to abide by a set of "privacy principles" in all of your data-handling practices:

- **Purpose Limitation:** You can only use personal data for the purpose for which it was originally collected.

- **Protection of Children's Data:** Fines are tripled when violating the privacy of children under sixteen, and permission from a guardian is needed for the collection of that child's data in the first place. And if you don't receive consent to collect a child's data, you have to wait twelve months before asking again.

- **Storage Limitation:** Data should be destroyed or deleted once the data has been used for its collected purpose.

- **Reasonable and Appropriate Security:** Security for

personal data must be appropriate for how sensitive
it is and the harm that would result because of unauthorized access.

One of the most significant features of the CPRA is its enforcement. While state attorneys general typically handle privacy cases—unless the FTC is involved, and even then, it's often a partnership—the CPRA established a new privacy regulator, the California Privacy Protection Agency (CPPA). The CPPA is a five-member board that can fine transgressors, hold hearings about privacy violations, and clarify privacy guidelines.

Other US State-Level Data-Privacy Laws

California, Utah, Virginia, Connecticut, and Colorado were the first US states to enact broad legislation that has had a national impact, but other US states have since passed data-privacy legislation, and many others are also actively considering data-privacy laws. There are over twenty states with inactive legislation that may be picked up again in the future or folded into new legislation.

I won't bog you down with the specific differences between state-by-state laws, but the resources on page 245 will point you to a guide on Osano's website that walks you through the key details. You'll find that many features are similar to what's found in the CPRA, such as the need to meet thresholds, consumer rights, and consent requirements. They often tend to differ in areas such as their threshold criteria, SRR coverage, fine amounts, and cure periods.

US Privacy Laws Enforced by the FTC

A final set of US laws to keep on your radar are the US privacy laws enforced by the Federal Trade Commission (FTC). The FTC's authority to regulate on behalf of consumer protections comes from the Federal

Trade Commission Act (FTC Act), which has broad jurisdiction over commercial entities under its authority to prevent unfair or "deceptive trade practices."[132]

The FTC uses its authority to issue regulations, enforce privacy laws, and take enforcement actions to protect consumers. For example, the FTC might take action against organizations that:

- Fail to implement and maintain reasonable data-security measures.
- Fail to abide by any applicable self-regulatory principles of the organization's industry.
- Fail to follow a published privacy policy.
- Transfer personal information in a manner not disclosed in the privacy policy.
- Make inaccurate privacy and security representations (i.e., lying) to consumers and in privacy policies.
- Fail to provide sufficient security for personal data.
- Violate consumer data-privacy rights by collecting, processing, or sharing consumer information.
- Engage in misleading advertising practices.

Other federal laws that govern the collection of information online include:

- The Children's Online Privacy Protection Act (COPPA), which governs the collection of information about minors.
- The Health Insurance Portability and Accountability Act (HIPAA), which governs the collection of health information.
- The Gramm-Leach-Bliley Act (GLBA), which governs personal information collected by banks and financial institutions.
- The Fair Credit Reporting Act (FCRA), which regulates the collection and use of credit information.

- The Family Educational Rights and Privacy Act (FERPA), which protects the privacy of student education records.

International Data-Privacy Laws

With data-privacy legislation in more than 130 countries across the globe, it isn't feasible to list and describe each and every one in this book. However, here are some important regulations that may apply to your business.

- **Brazil's General Law for the Protection of Personal Data, or the Lei Geral de Proteção de Dados Pessoais (LGPD):** This law went into effect in 2020 and contains many similar provisions to the GDPR. Some key differences, as outlined by GDPR.eu, are that the LGPD outlines ten legal bases for processing data while the GDPR outlines six; it provides an open-ended timeframe in which organizations need to report data breaches to the local data-protection authority whereas the GDPR requires breaches to be reported within seventy-two hours; and it issues lower fines than the GDPR.[133]
- **Canada's Personal Information Protection and Electronic Documents Act (PIPEDA):** PIPEDA was assented to in 2000, came into full force in 2004, and was considered a progressive law at the time. It was last updated in 2015 by the Data Privacy Act but still falls short of the GDPR's regulatory standard. One key difference between PIPEDA and the GDPR is consent. While the GDPR gives organizations six legal bases for processing data, consent is the only legal basis by which organizations can collect data under PIPEDA.[134]
- **China's Personal Information Protection Law (PIPL):** PIPL was enacted into law in November 2021 and broadly maps to the GDPR's stipulations. However, it does vary in some

of its details, notably by giving individuals fewer rights, requiring a stricter standard for consent, and imposing harsher penalties. A key element of the PIPL is that it does not limit China's government from accessing its citizens' data. This can be troubling from a government that is infamous for surveilling its people.

The Enforcement World

As you work on building your privacy program, it helps to be aware of what the enforcement world looks like, even if you aim to do everything right. Because even if an enforcement agency doesn't come knocking on your door, sloppy data-handling practices can be uncovered and lead to debilitating fines if an organization is caught not complying with regulations. The GDPR mandates one of the most significant fines. As we touched on earlier, organizations found to be in violation can be fined up to 4 percent of annual global revenue, or €20 million, whichever is greater. Other regulations may incur smaller fines, but the financial penalty, of course, isn't the only fallout of noncompliance. Rebuilding trust with customers can be a huge uphill battle that a company may never make it through.

Some required data-privacy practices are public facing and easier to spot, like how you handle cookie consent banners or SRR requests. Others are internal, like how well you protect customer data. Whether public or private, here are some of the ways that data-protection authorities tend to uncover noncompliance:

Data breaches: Even if a business is mostly compliant, flies under the radar of data-protection authorities, meets a minimum threshold of adequacy, or otherwise has data-privacy compliance imperfectly solved, data breaches pose a threat. Nobody can really control whether or not they become the target of cybercriminals. If your business controls or processes consumer data and that data isn't adequately protected, then a data breach will expose your consumers' data. As a result, data-protection authorities, plaintiff lawyers, or the state attorney general may find that you didn't meet the standards required by data-privacy regulations and are subject to enforcement.

Privacy rights groups: Data-privacy rights groups will sometimes assess the privacy practices of a sample of companies to determine whether they're complying with the law. If they find, for example, that a certain number of companies have manipulative cookie banners or deceptive privacy policies, they'll file a complaint with their relevant data-protection authority or with the attorney general.

Individual complaints: Data-privacy advocacy groups may have more resources and more time to spend on advancing a complaint, but individuals are just as capable of filing complaints with data-protection authorities or attorneys general. In all likelihood, these complaints would result from highly visible infractions, such as failing to provide consumers a choice to withdraw consent from cookies, failing to act on cookie consent choices, failing to act on SRRs, and so on. The odds are slim that any individual complaint will trigger enforcement actions, but they're never zero. As more complaints against the same company and for the same infraction build up, those odds increase.

Another important element to understand is *how* enforcement happens, and by whom. Again, there are a few channels through which it can occur:

Data-protection authorities (DPAs): For the time being, the majority of enforcement actions from data-protection authorities take place in the EU. When you hear about million-euro fines being levied against Amazon or Google, usually those were issued by an authority like the UK's Information Commissioner's Office (ICO), France's Commission Nationale de l'Informatique et des Libertés (CNIL), or Ireland's Data Protection Commission (DPC). Once made aware of a data-privacy violation, these organizations have the power to levy fines and penalties.

With the exception of the California Privacy Protection Agency (CPPA) enforcing the CPRA, the US lacks organizations specifically focused on privacy enforcement actions.

While a US federal data-privacy regulation has yet to be enacted into law, those bills that have been advanced in Congress generally plan to leave enforcement up to the FTC.

State attorneys general: In American states with data-privacy laws on the books, the state attorney general is the usual source of privacy enforcement actions. Attorneys general have the power to investigate a business merely under the suspicion that they are not complying with data-privacy regulations. If an attorney general discovers that a business is noncompliant, they'll typically issue a warning first. If that warning is ignored or isn't acted upon in a satisfactory way, state attorneys general will file suit.

Class-action lawsuits: Businesses can also face class-action lawsuits from plaintiff firms. The likeliest trigger for a class-action lawsuit will be a data breach—which, after all, is a highly visible public event that affects a class of people (i.e., the business's customers).

Private lawsuits: This is the least common means of enforcement, but it still bears mentioning. Most data-privacy regulations do not allow for what's called a "private right of action," meaning that individuals can't decide to sue businesses because they are not in compliance. However, there are some jurisdictions that permit a limited private right of action. The GDPR allows for a private right of action, but it isn't really designed for that purpose. In the EU, a private lawsuit would function differently depending on the laws of an individual member state. Moreover, the big, headline-grabbing fines wouldn't come about as a result of an individual lawsuit—only the data-protection authorities have the power to levy those kinds of penalties.

The CPRA also allows for a limited private right of action, but this only applies in the event of a data breach and only if certain types of consumer data were exposed.

Investigative sweeps: This is when a DPA or attorney general announces they're investigating a specific industry or a specific aspect of compliance. For example, in 2023 California Attorney General Rob Bonta announced an investigative sweep of large California employers, requesting information on the companies' compliance with the California Consumer Privacy Act (CCPA) with respect to the personal information of employees and job applicants.[135]

Putting It All Together

There's no question that the world of data-privacy regulations is . . . well . . . a lot. In addition to the regulations themselves, what your privacy program looks like will depend on factors like the size of your business, your geographic location, your industry, and whom you serve. Your program will also evolve as your company and regulations do. The rest of this book will walk you through the steps of building out your program.

But before you get to work on your program, I want to leave you with a framework for navigating the patchwork of privacy laws out there. These are the specific components you'll come across in different laws. As you determine which laws apply to you, look for these key factors.

1. **Which organizations are subject to the law, and which are exempt?** It isn't a matter of whether your headquarters is based out of a region with a data-privacy law or not—you might still be subject to one. These laws have specific criteria that govern which organizations are subject to or exempt from their regulations. Generally, this will

depend on the nature of your organization, the number of state residents or citizens that you collect data on, and whether you earn revenue from selling personal data. The exact figures differ from law to law, but most follow a similar pattern.

2. **Who is protected by the law?** Data-privacy laws will clearly define who and what they protect. Typically, laws will refer to a "consumer," "resident," or a "data subject." For the most part, these definitions will be fairly intuitive: data-privacy laws are meant to protect the real people who reside within a certain region, so that's who "consumer" or "data subject" refers to. To be safe, however, it's always best to look up the section of the law that defines the different terms it uses—every law will have a section dedicated to definitions.

3. **What constitutes personal information?** Most data-privacy laws will refer to "personal information" when discussing how businesses need to treat consumers' data. However, the meaning of "personal information" can vary from law to law. Generally, personal information is data that can be used to identify or can be reasonably associated with a consumer. Note that there are also exceptions to what constitutes personal information. Generally, data-privacy laws will exempt aggregated data or de-identified data. Aggregated data refers to data from groups of people that lacks any personally identifiable information, like website visits, bounce rates, and the like. De-identified data is similar but refers to data for which all personally identifiable information has been removed.

4. **What constitutes sensitive information?** Some data-privacy laws include an additional category of personal information: sensitive personal information. This includes

information like Social Security numbers, consumers' precise location, genetic data, and more. Data that falls under this category requires special treatment from businesses, such as requiring explicit opt-in consent prior to processing, special disclosures and notices, permitting consumers to ask that businesses limit the use of their sensitive information, and so on.

5. **What kind of consent do you need?** The type of consent and when and whether you need it vary by data privacy law. In some regions, you might need to gather consent before you can collect or process consumers' personal information. But the laws differ in how they define consent and what getting consent looks like. As we covered, there are generally two kinds of consent: opt in and opt out.

6. **What rights do consumers have?** Data-privacy laws list out the specific rights that consumers have in regards to their data. We covered some of them in this chapter.

7. **How are data transfers handled?** If your business collects personal information from consumers, then you probably share or sell that data with third parties. They could be software vendors, international partners, client organizations, and other groups. Data-privacy laws generally say that if you provide consumer data to a third party, then you're still liable for what that third party does with the consumer data. It doesn't matter if you do everything right; if the third party mishandles the consumer data, you'll be the one on the hook. Many data-privacy regulations provide recommendations for how businesses should handle data transfers, such as by putting certain contractual agreements in place. There is also guidance on how to handle international transfers since you might

transfer data from a region with one data-privacy law to a region with another law or no privacy law whatsoever.

8. **What are the penalties associated with breaking the law?** Data-privacy laws list out the fines and penalties businesses can expect to incur if they are noncompliant.

9. **Who enforces the law?** This may or may not be described in the actual text of the law itself, but it's essential for businesses to be aware of which authorities are enforcing a law.

TL;DR CHEAT SHEET

- Most current privacy regulations are based on the EU's General Data Protection Regulation (GDPR) that went into effect in 2018. The US still doesn't have a federal data privacy law, but states like California have instituted their own.
- The US privacy laws that do exist for consumer protection are enforced by the Federal Trade Commission (FTC) to prevent deceptive trade practices. Some other US laws include the Children's Online Privacy Protection Act (COPPA), the Health Insurance Portability and Accountability Act (HIPAA), and the Fair Credit Reporting Act (FCRA).
- The principles of the GDPR, upon which companies can model their privacy programs, are lawfulness, fairness, transparency, purpose limitation, data minimization, accuracy, storage limitation, integrity, confidentiality, and accountability.
- GDPR regulations largely focus on two key elements: how companies process personal information and data subject rights.
- Under the GDPR, organizations can only collect, store, process, or sell data if they can justify it with one of the following lawful bases: consent, contract, legal obligation, vital interests, public tasks, and legitimate interest.

- Data subject rights include the following: the right
  to be informed that you've collected and used personal data;
  the right to access that data and know how it's processed;
  the right to have incorrect or incomplete data rectified;
  the right to erase data or restrict the processing of PI;
  the right to data portability; the right to object to having
  their PI sold or shared; and the right to opt out of automated
  decision-making and profiling.

PART 2

Building Your Privacy Program

CHAPTER 6

A Bird's-Eye View of Your Privacy Program

M any companies don't have a strong data-privacy program simply because they don't know where to start. It's understandable. Teams are stretched thin; regulations are unfamiliar and intimidating; and often, it's not even clear what organizations need to do or who should be doing it.

Let's take the mystery out of the process. Developing a privacy program is a huge endeavor, but it doesn't have to be overwhelming. The next few chapters break down each element of building a program so you can work on it at your own pace. The advice here applies whether you're developing a privacy program from scratch, you already have one you'd like to update, or you fall somewhere in between. Wherever you are, know that your program will evolve as your company and regulations do. You'll never quite set it and forget it, but you can automate and streamline a lot. And once you have a clear sense of your goals and obligations, the whole endeavor won't be so intimidating.

Your first step is to understand what a data-privacy program actually is. Put simply, it's a framework through which you can find solutions to data-privacy problems. It's the collection of approaches, processes, and tools that you use to protect the privacy of your customers, employees, partners, and other stakeholders. Ultimately, it improves your organization's ability to collect, process, and store personal information in a way that complies with the relevant data-privacy laws. Data-privacy programs will differ from organization to organization, as every organization works with personal information in different ways. But so long as you focus on building a framework first, there are best practices and standards you can follow that will lead to a data-privacy program that works for your company.

It's also important to understand why you need a privacy program at all. The obvious reason is compliance. Nobody wants to get fined for breaking the law. Some folks wonder whether it would be more efficient and cost effective to ignore regulations and just pay a fine if they get caught. It's a fair question, and one we hear a lot. The reality is that most small- to medium-size businesses usually don't have the budget set aside for litigation if they do get tangled in a compliance mess. And although larger companies may have the resources to handle fines, noncompliance is usually not worth risking a company's reputation, no matter what size it is. Plus, the fines are substantial. In 2022, international beauty product retailer Sephora became the first target of California Consumer Protection Act (CCPA) enforcement when it was hit with a $1.2 million fine for failing to comply with regulations. In the EU, organizations that violate the GDPR can be hit with significant fines, as we've discussed.[136] With the eye-watering numbers we've seen, paying the fine may no longer seem like a sensible choice. In April 2023, Meta Platforms Ireland was issued a €1.2 billion fine following an inquiry into its Facebook service by the Irish DPC.[137]

Companies may wish to invest a fraction of such fines into proactively being compliant—and avoiding the reputational harm.

Remember, though, that the point of these regulations isn't to collect fines; it's to protect consumers and businesses. Compliance aside, a strong data-privacy program will help your company to:

- **Protect personal data:** Data-privacy programs help organizations protect the personal data of their customers, employees, and other individuals, which is essential for maintaining trust and confidence in an organization. Not to mention it's just the right thing to do.

- **Prevent data breaches:** Data-privacy programs help organizations prevent data breaches, which can result in serious harm to individuals and damage to an organization's reputation and financial stability. Today, data breaches are more common and more damaging than ever. According to the Identity Theft Resource Center, there are over eighteen hundred data breaches a year, impacting hundreds of millions of victims.[138] For businesses, data breaches can result in significant financial losses, damage to reputation, and legal consequences. Osano's own research shows that businesses with poor data-privacy practices are significantly more likely to be hit with a data breach.[139]

- **Improve business operations:** By understanding where consumer data lives and reducing the risk for data breaches, you also improve your overall information governance capabilities. As an ancillary benefit of your data-privacy program, you'll have cleaner, more up-to-date customer data and a better understanding of the data that is at your disposal.

- **Bolster your reputation:** Organizations with robust data privacy-programs are viewed as more trustworthy and responsible, which can enhance their reputations and increase customer loyalty.

Understanding these basics is a great start—although the path forward can still be confusing. It also doesn't help that there is not a one-size-fits-all template for creating a data-privacy program. In fact, no two programs will look the same from one company to the next. These challenges are paralyzing for so many companies, but they don't have to be.

A big part of our work creating privacy tools at Osano involves consulting with privacy experts, staying on top of current and upcoming regulations, and developing tools for companies worldwide to help them create their privacy programs. Although the companies we work with span a huge range of business types, models, industries, and geographic locations, we've found that the strongest data-privacy programs share similar elements. We've developed a framework that captures those elements and adapts to organizations' needs so they can create an agile program that will grow with them. It also takes the guesswork out of what to do, which is one of the biggest hurdles to building a data-privacy program.

The framework is made up of four simple pillars. We'll unpack each one in the chapters ahead so you can use them as a guide to create a new program or further develop one you may already have. Those pillars are:

Governance & Accountability (Chapter 7): A privacy program needs a team of advocates behind it and structured governance to guide the policies, procedures, and processes that the team will adopt. Creating them is the first step to building a program, and those charters keep evolving just as the company and regulations do.

Compliance, Audit & Review (Chapter 8): Organizations with strong privacy programs constantly review their activities and operations to make sure they're handling data as effectively as possible. This includes analyzing how they collect and store data, how they share data across departments and outside the organization, what their recordkeeping practices are, and whether they process data that is subject to specific permission or handling protocols. It's an ongoing effort, and companies should regularly look for opportunities to hone their practices along the way.

Notice, Consent & Choice (Chapter 9): Great privacy programs prioritize clear, direct communication with data subjects. They have systems in place that make it simple for data subjects to exercise their privacy rights; user-friendly consent banners; easy-to-find and easy-to-understand privacy policies; and a well-managed website that can house and support each of those features.

Risk, Response & Resilience (Chapter 10): There is always some level of risk involved when handling personal data, and those risks increase when a company shares personal data with third parties such as vendors. A strong program will have systems in place for assessing the risk associated with any of their operations. This includes vendor risk management, the risk of a data breach, and the risk of noncompliance within their internal data processes. Organizations should also have formal procedures in place for responding to SRRs and other potential data-related incidents.

As you dive into the next few chapters, you'll see how each of these pillars is essential to creating a privacy program that helps you stay compliant. But it's also important to know that building a privacy program won't always be a linear, step-by-step process. Sometimes you can develop multiple pillars in tandem. Other times, you'll need to develop one part of a pillar before you can develop part of another one. For example, you can't write your privacy policy, which is part of the Governance & Accountability pillar, until you go through the processes of data discovery and data mapping, as well as do a compliance audit, which are part of the Compliance, Audit & Review pillar. So I suggest reading these chapters before digging into the work. Understand what's needed, then work with your team to build out your program once you understand the pieces.

Your program will also have some surprising fringe benefits once you implement these pillars. It will streamline the way you process data and make a lot of your current tasks more efficient. And that will only keep happening as your program matures. Ad hoc data storage across various departments will become centralized and easily accessible, previously time-consuming tasks like answering SRRs can become nearly automated, and feelings of dread and being overwhelmed will no longer creep in at the sight or sound of the phrase "data-privacy compliance." And those are just the internal company benefits. As you gain confidence in your data-privacy practices, you'll be able to weave them into your company's identity as qualities that make yours a brand people can trust.

The Data-Privacy Program Life Cycle

In many ways, your privacy program is a living, ever-changing thing. It will develop at about the same pace your company does. That means creating and sustaining it is a continuous job. You'll always need to be aware of new privacy regulations and explore whether they're relevant to you; you'll always need to assess how your activities relate to data privacy; you'll always set new goals for growth so you can optimize and enhance your program in some way.

This life cycle of creating a data-privacy program offers an aerial view of the typical steps an organization cycles through as it builds its program. Together, these steps cover all four pillars while helping you keep an eye on the big picture. You can revisit this list any time and use it as a guide for creating or updating your program.

1. **Understand your privacy drivers.** Before you do anything, it's essential to learn all you can about the drivers behind your need for a data-privacy program. Understand the applicable data-privacy laws and regulations that apply to your operations, such as the GDPR or CCPA/CPRA. There might be other reasons why your organization needs a privacy program—such as reducing the risk of a data breach, building trust with your customers, and so on. Study these drivers as well and consider how they'll shape your privacy program. If you're updating an existing program, revisit the drivers you established when the program was created and determine whether there are new drivers your program needs to address.

2. **Establish a formal strategy.** Once you understand the specific requirements that your privacy drivers have, you can use the guidance in the chapters ahead to establish a formal strategy. Don't stress about having all of the answers when you start; your plan might involve a few steps where the plan is to investigate and plan further. Even if there are still gaps like these, it's important to show that you have a direction and a strategy to move ahead—this is especially crucial for the next step.

3. **Secure organizational buy-in.** You need commitment from the top levels of your organization in order to implement your privacy program. They're going to want to know what the organization stands to gain, how this will impact operations, how it will impact the budget, and so on. Most people who are not privacy professionals underestimate the amount of effort it takes to become compliant. Laying out the steps will help clarify and secure the resources

you need to be successful from the start. Furthermore, getting organizational buy-in will help you be more effective once your privacy program is live. If the whole organization understands that privacy is something they need to factor into their day-to-day responsibilities—such as team leads understanding the need to collaborate on SRRs or R&D understanding privacy-by-design principles—you'll be more efficient and better situated to scale. If you're making the case for an increased budget to update a current program, help your colleagues see how the developments would benefit all involved.

4. **Discover your data and conduct a RoPA.** Most businesses haven't had a reason to identify and track the personal data they collect until recently. As a result, many organizations have consumer data spread across multiple systems and databases. Discovering all of this data, classifying it, recording where it's going and where it came from, and more is crucial for all downstream compliance activities. If you don't know about it, you can't do anything about it. The GDPR refers to the classification and recording process as a record of processing activities (RoPA). Even if you aren't subject to the GDPR, following its RoPA guidelines is a good approach to this process.

5. **Conduct a privacy risk assessment.** Given the privacy drivers at play in your organization and the current state of your data-processing activities, where are you currently exposed to significant risk? You might discover that your security measures are not applied evenly across the organization or that you aren't able to quickly process requests to opt out of data collection. Flag these risk areas so you can prioritize controls to mitigate them.

6. **Establish goals and develop an implementation plan.** With a full sense of the scope of your privacy drivers, data-processing activities, and privacy risks, now you can identify the specific steps you need to take. That might involve identifying an SRR solution, revamping how your website secures consent, formalizing a vendor assessment process, and more. Almost certainly, you'll have multiple goals—it's important to prioritize based on the relevant regulations and your organization's biggest gaps. As part of this, you'll want to develop or update your privacy policy. Note that you may need a privacy policy for both customers as well as employees. Establishing your policies at this stage makes sense since you won't have the full picture of your data-processing activities before this step, and drafting a policy now forces you to consider what the day-to-day realities of your data-processing activities will be going forward. As a result, you'll have to account for the specifics of how your organization processes data. If you're updating an existing plan, consider whether any new practices or operations require you to update your privacy policies.

7. **Execute your implementation plan.** Once you have your plan, it's time to put it into practice. You'll need to implement technical and organizational measures to protect personal data, including encryption, access controls, consent management, vendor onboarding processes, incident response plans, and more. Make sure you include education and training in this step—privacy is not possible without collaboration and buy-in from across the organization, so you'll need to ensure your coworkers are equipped with the resources they need to comply with policies and procedures.

8. **Measure success.** After implementing the various
   technical and organizational measures contained in your
   data-privacy program, you'll want to see whether they
   work. Can you respond to an SRR within the thirty
   or forty-five days required by law? Does vendor onboarding take too long? Do your colleagues feel burdened
   and confused by the new data-privacy considerations
   they have to take into account? Measure and monitor
   these and other data-privacy metrics to identify whether
   you've been successful and how you can improve.

9. **Sustain and iterate.** Data-privacy laws and regulations
   are constantly evolving. Organizations need to stay
   up to date with the latest developments and changes
   in the legal landscape to ensure their data-privacy
   programs are compliant. Not only will the laws
   and regulations change, but your internal processes will
   change too. You'll collect and process data in new ways
   that may require data-privacy impact assessments
   (DPIAs) or other evaluations. And most significantly, your business will hopefully grow! As you grow
   larger, your data-privacy program will need to grow
   and evolve commensurately.

The Osano Privacy Maturity Model

(1) Reactive

Compliance activities are conducted in a reactive, one-off manner.

Consistency and Standardization. No consistency or standardization in how privacy issues are addressed.

Resources, Roles, and Responsibilities. Compliance is consistently underprioritized relative to regular business activities.

Monitoring and Improvement. Compliance is seen as a distraction from regular business.

Understanding of Data Privacy. Data privacy is perceived as an obstacle to be overcome and then quickly forgotten.

(2) Provisional

Some basic mechanisms for managing data privacy are in place.

Consistency and Standardization. Some standardization and consistency exists, though informally.

Resources, Roles, and Responsibilities. Compliance is a secondary responsibility held by non-privacy professionals.

Monitoring and Improvement. Occurs only in response to sudden development that brings privacy to the fore.

Understanding of Data Privacy. Privacy is understood to be important but is still perceived as a blocker.

(3) Formalized

The privacy program exists, and basic practices are documented.

Consistency and Standardization. A defined privacy program is in place and integrated into the organization's operations.

Resources, Roles, and Responsibilities. Privacy personnel have clear responsibilities; other functions' privacy responsibilities are not well understood.

Monitoring and Improvement. Semiregular reviews are conducted, but not acted upon.

Understanding of Data Privacy. Privacy implications are sometimes considered for new initiatives.

(4) Monitored

The privacy program is actively managed and assessed.

Consistency and Standardization. Policies and procedures are documented and applied consistently by privacy experts.

Resources, Roles, and Responsibilities. There are enough privacy personnel and resources to address the organization's compliance needs.

Monitoring and Improvement. The program is regularly reviewed to assess efficacy and identify gaps.

Understanding of Data Privacy. Leadership is aware of privacy-related activities. Privacy may be part of the organization's objectives and goals.

(5) Proactive

The privacy program is a central part of the organization's operations and strategy.

Consistency and Standardization. The entire organization consistently carries out compliance procedures.

Resources, Roles, and Responsibilities. Fully resourced with adequate budget, staffing, and authority.

Monitoring and Improvement. The program is continuously monitored to anticipate challenges before they arise.

Understanding of Data Privacy. Privacy is a key differentiator for the organization in the marketplace.

Our privacy maturity model is a useful framework to keep coming back to as you develop your privacy program. Your program will be a constant work in progress, which can feel like a blessing and a curse. On one hand, it helps to know that you don't need to perfect every part of your program on day one. But maintaining and maturing your program to meet evolving regulations, support operational challenges, and withstand external events can feel daunting and never-ending. To make this task more approachable, it helps to understand where you stand today and what you need to accomplish tomorrow to take your program to the next level.

We developed the Osano Privacy Program Maturity Model to help organizations better understand and benchmark their privacy programs and their growth trajectory. The model is a method for identifying how sophisticated your program is. It also lets you spot opportunities to grow your program over the long term. You can revisit the maturity model from time to time to see how your program is doing and how you can develop each of your program's pillars.

The following maturity levels can be applied to either the privacy program as a whole or to the individual privacy elements. Review these different levels and consider where your own privacy program and associated elements fall. You can find our more extensive maturity model document at osano.com/book. It offers more detail on each level and a scoring exercise to help you evaluate your privacy program.

Reactive: At this level, the privacy program or privacy element can't really be said to exist. Any privacy-related activities are conducted in a reactive, one-off manner, perhaps in response to a breach, major headline, or notice of noncompliance from authorities. Compliance is thought of as something that can be "solved" rather than a continuous process.

There is no consistency or standardization in how privacy issues are addressed. There may not be dedicated resources or budget for privacy activities. Factors such as compliance requirements; governing law; privacy risk; technical, procedural, and organizational measures to protect privacy; and so on are poorly understood.

Let's look at the maturity model levels through the example of SRRs, which are one of many privacy program elements. In practice, if a data subject sends an SRR to an organization with a reactive program, they would likely respond via email and manually track down the requested data by searching email and other company databases when needed.

Provisional: A privacy program or privacy element at a provisional maturity level has some standardization and consistency, though these may not be formalized or defined. Basic policies and procedures may be in place, but they are not fully integrated into the organization's operations. If there is a privacy professional or team working on these issues, they do not or are unable to collaborate much with other stakeholders, which limits their efficacy. The organization may have dedicated privacy resources and budget, but the program or element is restricted to a small sphere of operations within the organization. In essence, mechanisms for managing data privacy exist but are not fully documented and are not comprehensive.

In practice, if a data subject sends an SRR to an organization with a provisional program, the company might have a spreadsheet to help track down the subject rights request. But they're likely still using email for communication with both the subject and each department, and they're referring to the spreadsheet as and when needed. The organization could be perfectly compliant with a spreadsheet, but it would be easier to demonstrate the next level of maturity with a tool or centralized data source.

Formalized: At this level, the organization has a formal privacy program in place with well-defined policies, procedures, and standards that are integrated into the organization's operations. However, there may not be ongoing review and improvement to privacy-related procedures and processes. Data privacy is considered at the outset of new initiatives, and there are clear roles and responsibilities for privacy management that extend outside the spheres of strictly privacy-focused personnel.

In practice, if a data subject sends an SRR to an organization with a formalized program, the subject would be able to submit their request via a form and the organization would centralize all communications and workflows. However, only the privacy team would be using the tool.

Monitored: An organization with a monitored privacy program or element is actively monitoring, assessing, and improving the program or element. This level is characterized by a degree of proactivity not seen in the earlier maturity levels. Needs, challenges, regulatory updates, and more are considered in advance, and corresponding changes are made. Most importantly, processes and procedures are reviewed to assess their efficacy and identify gaps.

The broader organization is regularly kept informed of and involved in data-privacy issues. Senior management is particularly kept abreast of privacy-related activities, and data privacy may be a formal factor that contributes to the organization's objectives and goals.

In practice, if a data subject sends an SRR to an organization with a monitored program, the company's response will have become more automated than in prior maturity levels and each team would be actively using the tool to respond when automation isn't possible.

Proactive: At the highest maturity level, the privacy program or element is fully integrated into the organization. This maturity level is best characterized by ongoing, regular reviews and continuous improvement and/or adaptation.

The privacy program or element is continuously monitored and updated based on changes in the organization's operations and the privacy landscape. Privacy metrics and performance indicators are regularly tracked and reported to senior management, and privacy may be considered a key differentiator for the organization in the marketplace.

In practice, if a data subject sends an SRR to an organization with a proactive program, the response would leverage as much automation as is prudent. Other members of the organization and external vendors are aware of their need to contribute to the SRR response in a timely and complete fashion. Privacy professionals regularly review their SRR process in a proactive program, and each response serves as an opportunity to measure, test, and seek out new ways to be more efficient.

How to Use This Maturity Model

I want to emphasize that this maturity model is best used as a set of benchmarks to help you assess where your privacy program is and where it can go next. There are a few key points to keep in mind as you use it to analyze your program:

You do not have to be mature to be compliant. This maturity model is meant to help you understand how effective your organization is at operationalizing compliance. It does not measure compliance per se; what actually constitutes "compliance" will vary depending on your governing law, industry, unique organizational factors, and jurisdiction. It's possible that you could be perfectly compliant with a given law but still have a program at the reactive or provisional level. That would indicate that you're operating inefficiently and are at risk of expending too many resources and potentially falling out of compliance in the future. Having a program that's closer to the monitored or proactive levels indicates that it's sustainable, flexible, and using its resources effectively—not that it is compliant with this or that law.

Growing and scaling your privacy program is a journey. While privacy maturity models can be used to help identify potential compliance gaps, they primarily highlight operational challenges that limit efficiency or reduce effectiveness. Quick wins like moving from a spreadsheet maintained by a single person to a centralized tool can help scale, streamline, and automate—and lessen the risk of a single point of failure.

You do not have to obtain the highest level of maturity to be successful. Depending on your risk, you may choose to prioritize specific criteria to make incremental progress as time and resourcing permit. You may choose to accept a lower level of maturity in some areas that generate less risk for your organization and strive for a higher level of maturity in areas that present increased risk or operational challenges. Your privacy program should be tailored to meet your needs.

Revisit the Data-Privacy Program Life Cycle earlier in this chapter for guidance on the big-picture steps that go into building or updating your program. Do the same with this maturity model. As your business and the privacy landscape grow, come back to review the levels and see where you might be able to take a certain element to the next level.

TL;DR CHEAT SHEET

- If you think it's more cost-effective to ignore regulations and just pay any future fines, you should know that the damage to your reputation alone can kill your business. Also, fines are getting heftier, and creating a privacy program will be much more cost-efficient in the long term.
- A strong privacy program will protect PI, prevent data breaches, improve business operations, and bolster your reputation.
- A robust data privacy program has four pillars:
    1. Governance & Accountability.
    2. Compliance, Audit & Review.
    3. Notice, Consent & Choice.
    4. Risk, Response & Resilience.

- The steps for creating a data privacy program include understanding your privacy drivers, establishing a formal strategy, securing organizational buy-in, discovering your data, conducting a RoPA and a privacy risk assessment, establishing goals, developing and executing an implementation plan, measuring success, and sustaining and iterating the program.
- The Osano Privacy Program Maturity Model helps you benchmark your program and its growth trajectory along different levels of sophistication: Reactive, Provisional, Formalized, Monitored, and Proactive.
- Scaling your privacy program is a journey, and compliance can be attained at a lower level of the maturity model, with an option to work toward the highest operational efficiency.

CHAPTER 7

Governance & Accountability

A privacy program is only as strong as the people behind it. No company can do privacy well unless its top leaders support the program and actively participate in creating and sustaining it. The challenge is, many organizations need to work hard just to reach that point—and that's okay. It's common for privacy programs to have a sort of recruitment phase in which an individual or a small team of advocates works to convince their colleagues that they even need a privacy program. This is such a familiar hurdle because people often underestimate the complexity of data-privacy compliance. And that's if they understand why data-privacy compliance matters at all. The result is often small, under-resourced data-privacy programs—or nonexistent ones. So, as a first step, I'll help you build your team of advocates.

Just as important as the people is the governing framework that holds the privacy program together. These are the policies, procedures, and processes that an organization adopts to make sure its program is effective and compliant with relevant laws and regulations. They also clarify the ways in which its people are accountable for meeting the organization's privacy obligations. Given how confusing data-privacy compliance can be, strong governance is a team's lifeline for staying on top of privacy obligations. It can also help team members spot compliance gaps as operations and privacy regulations evolve.

Don't panic if you haven't formalized any sort of governing framework for your program yet or if there are no fellow privacy advocates in your company. Developing both is just part of the process of creating a strong program. Let's start with your people.

Getting (Almost) Everyone In

Here's how privacy programs originate in many companies: new or upcoming regulations land on someone's radar—perhaps a company's legal counsel—and a flag goes up that someone needs to start paying attention to this stuff. Often, one person gets tasked with figuring out what needs to be done. In a worst-case scenario, that person already has a full-time workload and is overwhelmed by the new responsibility. In a much better scenario, the company creates a new role so that someone is fully focused on handling privacy compliance. Wherever a company falls on this spectrum, those tasked with the job often face a universal challenge: privacy is relegated to one person or department. Their leaders and colleagues see privacy as that department's problem and something they don't need to think about. This makes it nearly impossible for privacy professionals to build a great program.

The reality is, a privacy program can't be strong without complete company buy-in since data privacy impacts so many different departments in an organization. Not only will you need your colleague's collaboration to carry out compliance activities, like developing a data inventory or executing an SRR, but some individuals might oppose the implementation of a data-privacy program out of fear that it will affect their work. The marketing department might express concerns over consent management and their ability to track leads. Your financial department might insist that there isn't room in the budget. Your CEO might think it's a waste of time to make privacy a company-wide mandate. An essential part of developing a data-privacy program is to secure buy-in from these and other stakeholders. You don't have to get 100 percent consensus—but you do need at least a champion or two and a general willingness to let you operate unimpeded.

You're reading this book, which means you care about your company's approach to data privacy. And you'll need to convince some key stakeholders in your company that they need to care too. Let's walk through an effective strategy for how to do that.

Recruit your allies.

To start, don't go straight to the C-suite. Eventually you'll need the buy-in of your organization's leadership, but it shouldn't be the first thing you seek. Instead, approach individuals who sit a level or two below any given leader. As an example, rather than the chief product officer, the head of engineering might be a better person to talk to first. These individuals may have more time to spare, and they'll be better able to identify stumbling blocks, privacy-adjacent activities they oversee, risks, goals, and so on. Armed with this information and hopefully with this individual's support, you'll be in a much stronger position when you do go to the C-suite and make your pitch.

Do your due diligence.

Make sure you actually know your organization's privacy posture before you get on anyone's calendar to discuss a program. Since privacy is so cross-functional, you'll need to understand every function in the business that handles personal information if you're to communicate key compliance initiatives to your colleagues. Don't put pressure on yourself to uncover everything about how your company handles data right now. That's a large project that actually makes up an entire pillar of your program, and we'll cover it in Chapter 8: Compliance, Audit & Review. For now, focus on the basics. Aim to show up to each conversation with an understanding of the key privacy laws your company is obligated to comply with and what the organization is currently doing—or not doing—to address those obligations. And be prepared to share what penalties the business is vulnerable to if it doesn't comply.

Also aim to figure out what you *don't know* about your company's actions related to data because you need others' help to figure it out. Some key points to uncover, either before your meeting or together with your colleagues, include:

- How data is collected in each department.
- How data the company has collected flows through different systems and to whom it is transferred.
- What technologies that the company is using rely on user data.
- What data-privacy processes are already in place.

This list isn't exhaustive, but it gets at the basics that are useful to know as you start to build or expand your privacy program. If you don't know the answers to these questions, bring them to your meetings with colleagues so you can talk them through together.

Define your goals and needs.

You're more likely to get buy-in if you link your needs and goals to tangible outcomes. Do you need an across-the-board budget increase? Will that budget be used for additional staff? For new tools? Do you need somebody to take on less important responsibilities so you can focus on the privacy program? Figure out where your gaps are and present a plan for how you want to plug them. The process of identifying your wants and needs can be a journey in and of itself, so it's important to start early.

Speak to each department's needs.

Each conversation with colleagues in various departments will go a little differently. It will be easier for your coworkers to get on board with privacy if you tailor your communication to their specific circumstances. It's important to talk about the fundamentals of data privacy, such as purpose limitation, consent, data minimization, and more, but those fundamentals need to be translated into actionable advice for the given audience:

- Marketing needs to understand why they must ask for data collection consent on the website, how to do it, and how it will impact their analytics data.
- Sales needs to understand when a tool may be processing prospects' personal information and why you need to be involved in an assessment.
- Development needs to understand how privacy fits into the development life cycle.
- HR needs to understand how privacy affects employees and candidates.
- The C-suite needs to understand the big picture, the cost,

and that the details are being handled by the people who understand them best.

Focus on what matters to them and their work and lean on relevant quantitative data when you can. For example, if you're speaking with folks in your finance department, they may be interested in knowing how much time and money current privacy operations cost the company and how much investing in your data-privacy program objectives could save. Does SRR fulfillment take you ten hours per week, when an automation tool could shrink that time to one hour and free you up to focus on tasks with greater ROI?

If you're speaking with someone in sales, consider asking them how often privacy comes up in conversations with prospective customers and clients. Even the occasional mentions could signify a larger demand for privacy protection amongst your target audience. If it doesn't come up, you can try to help your sales department see how integrating privacy into their discussions with prospects can make your company the more appealing choice.

When speaking with HR, you can ask whether employees reference privacy in internal pulse surveys or whether prospective hires have raised concerns.

Data around SRRs, in particular, may be relevant to people across several departments. Are they trending upward and therefore require better tooling and/or more staff to handle? Are there trends in key regions where the business operates? Is the business fulfilling SRRs on time or is it missing deadlines and inviting undue risk?

Also aim to keep tabs on—and communicate—the headlines. There's no shortage of news in Europe about major fines and penalties being levied out by data-protection authorities. Enforcement in the US is ramping up too, with Sephora's $1.2 million settlement in 2022 for violating the CCPA providing a major wake-up call to businesses that serve California residents. These headlines can be powerful motivators. They'll be even more powerful if you can point to businesses in your industry that have suffered data breaches—especially if the breach revealed noncompliance with a relevant data-privacy law. But remember, the goal isn't to persuade through fear; it's to provide an objective perspective into the nature of data privacy and the risks facing the business.

Turn blockers into advocates.

As you figure out whom in your company to approach about building your privacy program, take special care to target the blockers. Now, to be fair, unless they're already in the privacy world in some way, most people don't get too passionate about data-privacy compliance. That's okay, you can work with that. The real issue is when people are hostile to data privacy. Since most people feel neutral about privacy, blockers can be real momentum killers. Usually, blockers to your program will either be concerned about the financial impact on the business as a whole or the impact compliance will have on their ability to do their job. The former is often easier to assuage, as the cost of noncompliance can be a multimillion-dollar fine. The latter is a bit trickier. Often, the latter group is the marketing team. Marketing experts get worried that asking website visitors for data collection consent will interfere with their ability to analyze their audience.

If they're not persuaded by the fact that it's the law, then you might have more luck expressing how every business in your jurisdiction will have data collection consent banners on their website and that it will be an experience that website visitors expect to have. Or you could highlight the fact that people who opt out of data collection are less likely to be potential leads—they're signaling their disinterest straightaway, so why waste effort targeting those disinterested individuals with ads and emails?

Even if your biggest opponent isn't a marketer, they probably handle a lot of personal information in one way or another. These individuals are excellent people to talk to about recent enforcement actions, the particulars of the law, and the importance of data privacy as a right. They're the owners of risky processes—they just might not realize the scope of that risk until you communicate it.

If your biggest blockers are the individuals who handle the most personal information in your organization, you'll need them to be the most on board with your privacy program once it's up and running. After all, you'll likely be asking for their collaboration during privacy impact assessments, SRR fulfillment, and the like. That's why these individuals shouldn't just be passive nonobstructionists; they should care the most about data privacy. Marketing, HR, developers—working with personal information makes up a big part of how these people do their jobs. If they understand the risk created by personal information, the rights that need to be respected, and how it all translates into business and customer outcomes, they'll be the biggest advocates for implementing a data-privacy program that truly works.

By the time you've worked your way up to the C-suite, you'll ideally have enough team support for your program that top-level leadership will get behind it. You're essentially asking for two things from them: a commitment to the budget and resources you need and a top-level mandate that everyone in the organization participates in the privacy program.

Who's Doing What?

As the number of privacy advocates in your organization grows, you can begin to organize a leadership team. Aim to have at least one person from each department on the team so that it reflects a range of cross-company perspectives and functions. At the very least, folks from departments such as legal, IT, marketing, HR, and security should be represented since their work tends to intersect with personal data so directly. The more stakeholders across the organization who become involved, the easier it will be to secure necessary support as you work on building out your privacy program.

Create a charter for the hierarchy, roles, and responsibilities across the team. There is no one right way to structure your team, but a strong model could look something like this:

Executive-Level Members: They likely won't be in the weeds with day-to-day operations, but they're essential to making privacy a part of the company's culture by ensuring that it's treated as a strategic priority. You'll also likely need their approval on key factors like budget increases and new hires.

Privacy Leaders: These are the privacy experts who are steering the program. They're familiar with the laws and regulations that are relevant to the organization and play a major role in establishing and overseeing the privacy program's governing framework.

Privacy Champions: You'll need a champion on every nonprivacy team who is accountable for making privacy a priority in whatever their department is doing. This is especially important in departments like sales, marketing, or IT that rely on or access user data in most of their work.

Privacy Working Groups: These are core working groups that are responsible for making sure the company commits and executes on required action items related to a project, law, or regulation. For example, if your organization needs to begin complying with the CPRA, this group would work closely with each department and examine each of the company's functions to make sure they align with the new obligations. You might also form a working group around a new initiative, like the adoption of a new CRM platform. In this case, you may want to involve someone from every department in the process so they can weigh in on items related to their jurisdiction. Someone from legal, for instance, would advise on what the contract should look like; someone from sales would advise on what the customer journey should look like; someone from IT might advise on administration; and so on. The roles would depend on the nature of the project and how privacy heavy it is.

Ultimately, your privacy team will work together to build your privacy program and integrate it into your company culture and operations. Key actions they'll take to do this include:

- Understanding your organization's geographical footprint so you can determine what laws, regulations, customs, and cultural norms may be applicable.
- Embedding champions across departments to act on your privacy program's initiatives and gather feedback on how to successfully operationalize your program.
- Determining what compliance requirements need to be operationalized and aligned with processes, such as performing privacy impact assessments and fulfilling SRRs.

You'll learn and evolve together, along with your privacy program, so put one foot in front of the other and aim to support one another as you go.

Create Your Privacy Policy

Once your privacy team is in place, an essential next—and ongoing—step is to develop your privacy policy. As consumers, we're all familiar with privacy policies. Every one of us, at some point, has been prompted to accept the terms of a website's privacy policy or acknowledge when one has been updated. And let's face it: we rarely read them. That is, unless we're concerned about a privacy issue. When that's the case, a company's privacy policy is usually the first place we turn to.

A privacy policy plays two major roles in your privacy program:

1. **It's the program's governing document**, outlining all the ways in which the organization accesses user data and what they plan to do with it. This governing document functions as a blueprint for your privacy program and is publicly available to regulators, customers, and all website visitors. Your organization is obligated to abide by everything outlined in its privacy policy.

2. A well-crafted privacy policy also serves as **a tool for building trust** with anyone who engages with your organization. It demonstrates that you respect their privacy and will treat their data responsibly, reduces your risk exposure in the event of a data breach or lawsuit, and demonstrates to third parties that you meet their data-privacy standards and are therefore a reliable partner. In other words, it communicates your organization's values and goals.

Privacy policies are so all-encompassing that developing one can feel like a monumental task. Even if your company already has one (and it would be surprising if it didn't), you'll need to revisit every part of it as you build your privacy program to make sure the policy and your program align. It's a big project, and I'll walk you through everything you and your team need to consider when creating one in the privacy policy checklist ahead. But before we dig into the details of what to include, it's important to approach your privacy policy with these big-picture ideas in mind:

Don't just copy-paste. Since your business, your industry, your vendor relationships, your data processes, and your governing jurisdiction are all unique to you, you can't just copy-paste somebody else's privacy policy. Some of the basic information common to all privacy policies can be lifted and shifted, but realistically, it's best to just draft your own policy that contains the pertinent details of your business based on the privacy policy checklist in this chapter.

Privacy policies are mandatory and enforceable. If you operate within or have users within a jurisdiction with a data-privacy regulation, you're legally required to include a privacy policy or an equivalent disclosure on your website or application. Article 13 of the General Data Protection Regulation (GDPR), for instance, doesn't explicitly mention a privacy policy but does assert that "the controller"—that's you—"shall, at the time when personal data are obtained, provide the data subject with all of the [relevant privacy] information."[140] You don't have to communicate this info in a privacy policy per se, but it really is much more convenient to keep a dedicated page or channel covering all the required privacy information—i.e., a privacy policy. Section 1798.130 of the CPRA, on the other hand, does explicitly require a privacy policy.[141]

Other states and countries have similar stipulations, either implicitly (like the GDPR) or explicitly (like the CPRA). What's more, privacy policies aren't just guidelines—you have to do what you say you do in your privacy policy. If not, you're liable to face enforcement actions from the FTC, EU data governance authorities, and other organizations, depending on your users' geography.

Think broadly. Say you're a small business that only sells products in California. Obviously, you'll want to craft a privacy policy that complies with the CPRA, but you may think that it's not necessary to comply with regulations like the Virginia Consumer Data Protection Act (VCDPA), let alone South Africa's Protection of Personal Information Act or the EU's GDPR. This approach, however, could be shortsighted. Once you have customers, users, or data subjects in any of those jurisdictions and meet the applicability requirements—even if your business isn't located within them—then you are still beholden to those regulations. So it makes sense for you to plan ahead.

Fortunately, most regulations have significant overlap. When in doubt, adhere to the GDPR and the CCPA/CPRA at a minimum, as these are broadly considered to be the gold standard of data-privacy regulations. Also be sure to check on whether you're responsible for adhering to any industry-specific regulations.

Double-check with legal counsel. If you follow the privacy policy checklist in this chapter, you'll be in a fairly strong position. It includes information required by most major data-privacy regulations. However, the best way to minimize risk is to consult with legal experts who understand the relevant laws and regulations that apply to your business.

Privacy Policy Checklist: What to Include in Your Policy

This checklist captures all the elements that a strong privacy policy should include. You'll need to work through the remaining three pillars in this book to get a clear sense of how you'll handle most of what's listed here, but this is a framework you can come back to as you begin to formalize and articulate each part of your program.

1. **Your business and contact information.** First and foremost, your privacy policy should include your organization's full name, address, and any other contact information you can provide. If you have a data-protection officer

(DPO) or an equivalent individual at your organization, you should provide their information as well.

Note that under the GDPR, a DPO is required if you process sensitive data on a large scale or monitor individuals on a large scale. Hospitals, security companies, and the like are good examples of organizations that need a DPO. For more specifics on the GDPR DPO requirement, see Article 37 of the GDPR.[142] Even if you don't meet those requirements, keeping a dedicated professional with designated privacy responsibilities on staff isn't a bad idea.

2. **The categories of data you collect.** Describe the categories of personal information collected, sold, shared, and disclosed within the preceding twelve months as well as details about what types of personal information you collect from users. This could include, among other details:

- Personal identifiers, such as names, email addresses, identification numbers, and the like.
- Geolocation data.
- Demographic data, such as race, gender identity, age, and the like.
- Internet activity data.

Different regulations have different categories of data that you should disclose. When in doubt, try to follow the CPRA's guidance, which requires that categories of collected data must be disclosed in privacy policies and asks companies to discuss the information they obtain "in a format that is easily understandable to the average consumer."[143] Additionally, it's a good idea to disclose that you do not collect the personal information of minors, if that's the case. If you do collect the personal information of minors, you should seek legal counsel's help in making sure you are handling that data and the disclosure properly.

3. **The sources of the data or how you collect data.** Describe how you collect or source data, including a description of the categories of sources. While you likely collect some information from the user directly, it's possible you collected information from a third party, such as government databases, internet service providers, advertising networks, and so on.

4. **The purpose of data collection.** What do you intend to do with your users' data? It could be for fraud prevention, a better customer experience, marketing purposes, or any other reasonable use case for user data. It's also a good idea to delineate the purpose behind each category of personal information that you listed in item two of this list. If you don't have a good reason to collect a given category of data, then most data-privacy regulations require you to not collect it at all. Note that if you intend to use personal information for targeted advertising, many regulations require you to clearly and conspicuously disclose that fact as well as the fact that the consumer can opt out of this processing. Most major privacy laws also require that you disclose whether consumer data will be used in automated decision-making processes, how consumer data impacts this decision-making, the associated results and consequences, and the users' right to opt out of that decision-making. Often, these automated processes can include an element of bias, a reality that these laws try to mitigate with this requirement.

5. **The legal basis of data collection.** You'll also want to take note of your legal basis behind data collection. The GDPR, for instance, lists out the following as acceptable legal bases for collection:

- User consent (which is the most common basis used today).
- A contractual obligation.
- A legal obligation requiring your organization to process user data (e.g., a lawsuit or subpoena issued by a governmental entity).
- Vital interest: that is, that processing the user's data is necessary to preserve life, safeguard fundamental rights, support humanitarian emergencies, and other select circumstances.
- Public interest.
- A legitimate interest in processing the user's data (another commonly used basis, though you'll need to disclose the nature of your legitimate interest).[144]

6. **The consumer's rights.** Make sure you clearly describe the rights the user (or data subject) you are collecting data from possesses and how they can exercise these rights. These can vary from regulation to regulation, but generally, data subjects have:

- The right to access personal information.
- The right to rectify incorrect personal information.
- The right to object to the processing of personal information.
- The right to withdraw consent to the processing of personal information.
- The right to lodge a complaint with a supervisory authority (which varies depending on where the data collection occurs).
- The right to appeal a business's decision with regard to a data subject's request.
- Other rights depending on your and your users' jurisdiction.

7. **Who you share personal information with.** Your privacy
   policy should disclose whether or not you sell personal
   information, whether you have sold personal information in the last twelve months, and which categories
   of personal information you have sold. Under the CCPA,
   you only had to disclose if you sold data—that changed
   under the CPRA, which stipulates that you disclose both
   shared and sold data.

   If possible, provide the specific details of the recipient.
   Under the CCPA/CPRA, you also have to inform your
   users about which categories of recipients you sell their
   data to or share their data with (e.g., suppliers, credit
   reference agencies, government departments).

8. **Whether the data will be transferred across borders
   and how.** Transferring data into another country or state
   can expose your users' data to greater risk. If you operate
   out of California or the EU, for instance, and transfer
   data to a jurisdiction with less robust data-protection
   laws, the recipient may treat your users' data with less than
   the respect it deserves.

   However, it's possible to establish safeguards to enable
   a compliant data transfer. Typically, this takes the form
   of a contractual agreement (such as the GDPR's Standard
   Contractual Clauses) between your organization
   and the receiving party affirming that they will treat your
   users' data to the same standards as you do.

9. **Whether data collection is voluntary or mandatory.** Indicate what categories of data that you collect
   are required or are optional. If your users decline to share
   data that would be useful for marketing and analytics
   purposes, they can still use your website, make a purchase,
   use your app, or engage in whatever other activity serves

as the focal point of your relationship. On the other hand, if you operate an e-commerce business and they refuse to share their address with you, you won't be able to ship them the products they order. Depending on the nature of your organization, the type of data that needs to be collected in order to serve your users will vary.

10. **Your data retention policies.** How long do you intend to retain the different categories of your users' data? If you're uncertain about the exact answer, under what circumstances will you no longer need a user's data? Explain what criteria you will use to determine when you'll delete that data.

11. **Your security measures.** Certain regulations require that you state your security measures in a privacy policy, while others merely require that you maintain them—in any case, it's still a good idea to include them in your privacy policy. This builds trust with your users and signals that you take their privacy seriously. You might indicate whether you pseudonymize and/or encrypt personal data, whether you can back up and restore data in the event of an emergency, whether you comply with security standards like SOC 2, and more.

12. **Your financial incentive programs.** If you provide a financial incentive, a price difference, or a service level difference based on a user's data choices, you have to include what's called a "Notice of Financial Incentive" under the CCPA/CPRA. This disclosure needs to contain:

- A brief summary of the program.
- A detailed description of the program.
- Info on how the consumer can opt in.
- A right of withdrawal.[145]
- An explanation of the value provided by the program.

13. **How you will communicate changes to your policy.** As your organization evolves and laws change, your policies will too. Tell consumers how you'll let them know about future changes to your data management plan.

14. **Effective date.** Was your data-protection strategy updated a week ago or a decade ago? Show full transparency by including the effective date of your current privacy policy.

Pro Tip: Make Your Privacy Policy Easy to Understand

Unfortunately, the majority of privacy policies on the web are a confusing mishmash of legalese and technical jargon. In fact, according to one analysis based on readability metrics like sentence length and complexity, Facebook's privacy policy was only slightly easier to read than Immanual Kant's infamously dense *Critique of Pure Reason*.[146]

Do your users a favor and spend time crafting a privacy policy that anybody can understand. It's not just a nice thing to do: when users understand what you're doing with their data, they're more likely to do business with you and less likely to make complaints or leave negative reviews should they make an unexpected discovery. What's more, spending time to write a clear privacy policy is actually an activity that brings you closer to compliance. Article 12 of the GDPR stipulates that privacy policies must be delivered "in a concise, transparent, intelligible and easily accessible form, using clear and plain language, in particular for any information addressed specifically to a child."[147]

If you follow the guidance in this privacy policy checklist, you'll be on the right track when it comes to clarity, but there's always room for improvement. If you're looking for inspiration, visit osano.com/book for some notable privacy policies that we think do a great job of including all the requisite information in an easy-to-understand way.

The Bottom Line on Your Privacy Policy: Do What You Say You'll Do

More important than having a comprehensive privacy policy is actually doing all the things you promise within it. Adhering to your privacy policy will help you keep your organization secure, improve your data governance practices, and keep you in compliance.

Training & Awareness

I'll say it again: a privacy program is only as strong as the people behind it. Having a robust privacy policy is essential for making all stakeholders aware of your company's privacy posture and practices. But your privacy team's work doesn't stop once that policy is posted to the company website. They need to ensure that the practices outlined in your policy are carried out daily, across all departments. That's a tall order—especially since some data custodians across departments will have more knowledge than folks on the privacy team of intricate processes or systems that process data. Those data custodians need to become privacy champions, and really, the whole company needs to be aware of your firm's privacy practices. That's where training and awareness come in.

Your privacy team will play a lead role in educating colleagues on your privacy program and its importance. Here are some key factors to keep in mind as you're creating your training and awareness program:

- Tailor training to specific jobs and levels within the organization.
- Emphasize why responsible data handling is so important: it's not only the law; it's the right thing to do.

- Share your organization's privacy policy and relate policy elements to different stakeholders' roles and responsibilities.
- Design a process that you can consistently roll out to all employees (including new hires), contractors, consultants, and other workers with access to data and/or company systems.
- Explore different training methods to address your organization's unique education needs.
- Identify the best means of delivering training within your budget, such as e-learning modules or recorded trainings, in-person training sessions, and simulations.
- Find ways to make training fun and engaging. You can develop interactive quizzes, host games with prizes, create a shared playlist, send a newsletter, or anything else that educates your colleagues on the importance of privacy while keeping them engaged.
- Remember that privacy is an evolving space, so you'll need to update your training as privacy issues, regulations, and technologies evolve.

Remember: you can't expect your team to get it all right from the start. But do start. Get your training program off the ground and then measure and iterate over time. You can work to strengthen your training by testing colleagues to evaluate the efficacy of the program, report on results, and identify gaps in both the organization's knowledge of privacy-related topics as well as the training materials. Also report on KPIs, metrics, training outcomes, and risks to senior leaders so that they have oversight of the program and insight into training needs.

Over time, ongoing privacy training and awareness will contribute to a strong culture of privacy throughout your organization, but they're not mutually inclusive. A robust training and education process contributes to a culture of privacy but does not guarantee it.

The degree to which your organization adopts a culture of privacy will depend in part on your colleagues' personalities, the industry you operate within, and the products and services your organization provides. The culture surrounding privacy issues at your company can be the X factor that elevates your privacy program to new heights. Because data-privacy activities are often interdisciplinary and interdepartmental in nature, other stakeholders' understanding of and attitudes toward privacy will have a major impact on privacy professionals' ability to do their jobs. In an organization with a mature privacy culture, the work becomes much easier; in an organization with an immature or absent privacy culture, executing basic tasks can feel like herding cats. You can get there—and the work starts with a strong team, a strong privacy policy, and strong education across the company.

TL;DR CHEAT SHEET

- Your privacy program is only as strong as the people behind it. Get buy-in by recruiting allies, doing due diligence, and defining the privacy needs and outcomes for each department (such as marketing, sales, product development, HR, and C-suite).
- Most people are neutral toward privacy, so pay special attention to turning blockers into advocates because they can and will kill your momentum (the two main issues to address are added costs and inefficiencies). Spoiler: You'll likely receive the most hostility from the marketing department.
- Your two big asks from your C-suite are the budget and resources to implement the program and a top-level mandate that everyone in the organization participates in the program.
- Create a privacy program leadership team that includes a representative from each department (but at least legal, IT, marketing, and HR). This team should be composed of executive-level team members (who handle the big-picture, company-wide strategy), privacy leaders (who handle the on-the-ground implementation and oversight of the program), privacy champions (who make privacy a priority on other teams), and privacy working groups (who focus on privacy pushes related to specific projects, laws, or new regulations).

(continued...)

- Create a privacy policy that plays two major roles in your privacy program. First, it's your program's governing document that's publicly available for regulators, customers, and website visitors. Second, it serves as a tool for building trust.

CHAPTER 8

Compliance, Audit & Review

This pillar of your privacy program helps you wrangle all the data your company collects and then keep it organized. The steps here will also keep you aware of the laws and regulations that are relevant to your company, give you a clear view of your current data practices, and help you figure out whether you need to change any of those practices to stay compliant.

Compliance, Audit & Review is a fundamental part of creating a privacy program since you can't do much with the other three pillars until you know what's going on with your data and what your related compliance obligations are. You'll get a basic sense of your organization's privacy posture when you do your due diligence before recruiting privacy allies. But like I mentioned in the last chapter, you're limited in how much you can discover at that point because it's nearly impossible for one person to uncover all the ways in which a company interacts with data across departments. It's especially difficult if an organization doesn't have data-privacy tools in place or a data-protection officer (DPO) to help with the task. Most companies have huge amounts of data in systems scattered throughout their organization. There's usually a lot to uncover and organize.

If you're doing this for the first time, it can feel like an insurmountable job. You need to figure out every place your company collects data, where they store it, what they do with it, and what they potentially should be doing with it instead. It's a lot, so this chapter breaks it down into manageable, repeatable actions that you can use to build your program and then revisit to keep your privacy practices optimal over time. Those actions are:

Compliance first look: Before you analyze your data practices, determine which major privacy laws and regulations apply to your organization. This is just a cursory look at your compliance obligations. After you organize your data through data mapping, you'll revisit compliance in greater detail.

Data mapping: This is the process of identifying all the data that your company collects and stores and organizing it into what's known as a data map. At a basic level, data mapping involves charting the source, flow, and destination of data. It identifies personal information across systems, then assembles it in one place so you can easily find, track, and protect it.

Compliance deep dive: Once you have a better handle on your data, you can revisit your obligations to figure out what actions you need to take to stay compliant based on your data-handling practices. You'll figure out your approach and requirements for essentials such as disclosures, contracts, SRRs, and vendor monitoring.

After your program is up and running, make this process routine. Review your program and practices at regular intervals to determine whether you need to comply with any new regulations that may have emerged and ascertain that your practices are still optimal.

Ideally, you'd have a DPO to direct your program and this process. The GDPR requires certain organizations to have a DPO, but even if your company doesn't need one by law, it's an excellent practice to have one if you can. Essentially, a DPO serves as a liaison between data subjects—any person on whom an organization collects data—and the organization's main supervisory authority. They'll focus on verifying a company's compliance with relevant privacy laws and facilitate connections among data subjects, regulators, and C-suites. The DPO also monitors a company's data processing and performs data-protection impact assessments (DPIAs), which we'll cover shortly.

Regardless of who is spearheading your data-privacy program, these steps will help you figure out where your organization stands and what it needs to do next to stay compliant and ahead of the curve.

Compliance First Look

To start, establish context by determining which laws apply to your organization. Data-privacy laws vary depending on the jurisdiction, and many laws only apply to certain businesses. For example, even if you run a Utah-based organization, there's a chance you still have to comply with California's CPRA. If you run a California-based organization, for that matter, you may have to comply with Utah's Consumer Privacy Act (UCPA). Privacy laws also exist for particular industries and data sets, such as HIPAA for anyone handling health-related information and COPPA for organizations that handle children's data. You can revisit Chapter 5 for a rundown of some of the most ubiquitous privacy laws. We also recommend working with a data-privacy expert to help you uncover any other laws or regulations that may be relevant to your organization.

As you research your compliance obligations, consider factors such as:

- **Company locations:** Where do you have a physical presence? What geographic areas does your company serve beyond its physical location, either through its online presence or in other ways?
- **Industry-specific requirements:** Are there regulations specific to your industry?
- **Data sharing:** Do you transfer data you receive from customers to other entities?
- **HR & finance compliance:** Are you collecting data that requires additional consents or additional data handling?

Don't worry if you're not sure about some of these—you'll uncover your data-handling practices in the next two steps. Also keep in mind that, even if you aren't subject to a given data-privacy law, you might still want to implement its requirements. Doing so will ensure you're respecting your customers' data rights and set you up to gain customers in that jurisdiction in the future.

Data Mapping

Data mapping is where the truth comes out. That may seem scary, but it's a good thing. So much of the stress around data-privacy compliance is connected to unknowns. Companies don't know what data they collect, where it is, and what the implications are when they shine a compliance light on their data practices. And a lot of stress is linked to that disorganization. In a global 2021 survey by the International Association of Privacy Professionals, 47 percent of respondents said that the most difficult part of responding to SRRs was locating an individual's data within the organization.[148] In other words, the request itself wasn't the problem; it was getting their ducks in a row to be able to provide the basic information that they were obligated to share.

This is where data mapping comes in. Data mapping is a set of activities aimed at producing a complete picture of all the personal information your company collects. The process produces two key outputs: a data inventory and a data map.

A **data inventory** is a list of all personal information an organization collects and stores along with any information needed to manage that data.

A **data map** is a visual representation of the information in your data inventory. It documents where a data set came from and where it goes, giving you well-organized and structured records of your data that are easily accessible. This is essential for GDPR compliance. Ironically, the term "data mapping" is not mentioned in the GDPR, so some folks argue it's not truly mandatory. However, the GDPR does require nearly all businesses to meet requirements like creating records of processing activities (RoPA), fulfilling SRRs, and conducting data-protection impact assessments (DPIAs). Complying with these requirements is possible without data mapping but exponentially more challenging and time consuming.

Since your data map relies on your data inventory, the best way to get started is to do a thorough inventory of your data. Here are the essential elements we suggest tracking so you can fulfill SRR, RoPA, and DPIA requirements, among other obligations:

1. **What data you're collecting.** You should have a good grasp of the data you're collecting. Is it names, addresses, locations, local identifiers, sensitive information, or something else entirely? Document everything even before you start the data-mapping process.
2. **Who is responsible for managing the data.** Somebody

should be accountable for the data. Ideally, this person would be able to confirm all of the details about the data that you need for data inventory and mapping.

3. **What your data sources are.** Be sure to account for all sources of data collection, not just the most visible ones.

4. **Where you're storing the data.** This is one of the most important questions, especially when it comes to fulfilling SRRs. The answer might become complicated if you use multiple data stores.

5. **Whether you transfer the data.** If so, where does it go? Look at internal transfers and especially at external ones. If data is crossing borders, particularly to non-EU countries, this step will be even more important in helping you achieve GDPR compliance.

6. **The purposes behind the data processing.** Remember that you need consent from the users in most cases. Ideally, you'll only process data for strictly necessary purposes to reduce the risks of data breaches and to simplify compliance.

7. **How long you retain the data.** Last but not least, you need to know exactly how long you'll be processing and storing the data. The duration is not necessarily part of data mapping, but answering this question will help you reduce your risk.

8. **Whether you share data with vendors or third-party organizations.** Understanding what data goes to which vendor allows you to decide how to treat each data set. Ultimately, it's your responsibility to vet how vendors treat (and pass on) the data you've collected.

Be sure to make data mapping a regular practice. It's something you should do again and again, refining your process or analyzing data from different angles.

Once you've gone through the data-mapping process at least once, you'll be able to:

- Know where personal data is stored and when it's processed, at all times.
- Have clear evidence of the types of data you collect.
- Know what categories of data you have, including whether you work with sensitive data that is subject to additional restrictive provisions that you must adhere to.
- Know who can access your data and when.
- See how long you store personal data.

And you'll quickly drop the headaches that go hand in hand with trying to manage data-privacy compliance. Instead, you'll be on your way to knowing everything that's happening with the data in your organization.

Rocking Your RoPA Requirements

The GDPR requires all businesses with over 250 employees to keep a **record of processing activities (RoPA)** as outlined in the regulation's Article 30. Think of your RoPA as a snapshot of your data-processing practices. It's a single document that outlines all of your business's data-processing activities. Some examples of processing activities include HR, recruiting, managing payroll, marketing, or third-party activities that process personal data. Make no mistake, a RoPA is not the same as a data map, although it will be more difficult to generate a RoPA if you don't have a data map first. A RoPA builds on your data map by going into further detail about your data-processing activities.

While keeping records of processing activities is legally required by the GDPR for most businesses, it is also a helpful tool for self-auditing and evolving your program. Maintaining and understanding these records is essential for companies as they seek to identify processing risks. Once you know the risks, you can develop a plan to mitigate them.

The GDPR requires every business, regardless of its number of employees, to maintain a RoPA if:

- Your processing is likely to result in a risk to the rights and freedoms of data subjects.
- You process data frequently.
- You process special categories of personal data, including race, gender, sexuality, religion, and others.[149]
- You process personal data relating to criminal convictions and offenses.

Using these benchmarks, almost every organization is required to keep a RoPA.

Because RoPAs and GDPR data mapping go hand in hand, the requirements in Article 30 will have a big influence on your data-mapping approach. Article 30 lays out all requirements for maintaining RoPAs. Records of processing activities kept by a data controller should include:

- The name and contact details of the data controller.
- The purpose of processing the data.
- Categories of the data subjects and types of personal data.
- Categories of data recipients, including those who have already received a user's data and those who will receive a user's data in the future.
- Transfers of data to a third country or an international organization.
- Time limits for erasure of different categories of data.
- A general description of technical and organizational security measures.

Additionally, data processors must maintain records on behalf of all data processed for the controller. This RoPA should include:

- Each processor's name and contact details and the name and contact details of each controller that has engaged them to process the data.
- The categories of processing carried out on behalf of each controller.
- Transfers of data to a third country or an international organization.
- A general description of technical and organizational security measures.

You'll already be on your way to capturing these details if you include the eight elements in your data map that I shared on page 169. As you drill down to more specific details in your data map, make sure it captures the extra layer of information outlined here so that your RoPA requirements are covered. The French supervisory authority, the Commission Nationale de l'Informatique et des Libertés, shares an example of a RoPA on their website. We also offer a sample RoPA at osano.com/book.

All this said, a RoPA should be concise and easy to read. It should also be updated any time your procedures for processing information change. Finally, keep in mind that Article 30 states that all organizations legally required to keep RoPAs should be ready to present the record to supervisory authorities upon request. In case of an audit or in the aftermath of a data breach, supervisory authorities may ask you to submit additional evidence. Additional information may include records of consent, privacy policies, contracts, and other relevant data.

Demystifying DPIA Requirements

Data-protection impact assessments (DPIAs) are another common requirement. They rely heavily on data mapping, so it's a good idea to keep DPIA parameters in mind when setting up your data map.

A DPIA is a risk assessment audit designed to help organizations identify, analyze, and minimize the privacy risks that come with handling user data. The GDPR mandates DPIAs for processing that poses a high risk to a person's rights and freedoms or for certain large-scale processing of personal data. But there's one problem with that guidance: there is no clear definition for "large scale" or "high risk" set out in the GDPR. Given this lack of specific guidance, it's a good practice to conduct a DPIA for any major project that requires the processing of personal data.

DPIAs aren't meant to be an afterthought; they're an integral part of keeping your customers' information private and protected. They also tie into a key aspect of the GDPR legislation: the principle of "privacy by design." The idea behind "privacy by design" is that technical and organizational measures to protect consumer data should be built into business applications and processes that handle that data.

As a means of achieving privacy by design, a DPIA is recommended any time a company creates a new product or feature that will collect or process personal information in a new or different way. This enables privacy by design—before an organization can build a new product or feature, DPIAs ensure that the privacy needs are considered first rather than bolted on afterward. The findings in the assessment should then be used to consider and implement protections to mitigate the impact on an individual's privacy.

Organizations that perform data-processing activities and that must comply with the GDPR should plan to make DPIAs a part of their workflows. If you need help starting out, you can reference the UK ICO's page on DPIAs (search "DPIA" at ico.org.uk), which includes guidance and a DPIA template.[150] A DPIA should include the following:

- Whose data you are processing.
- What kind of personal information you will use.
- A description of the nature, scope, and context of the processing.
- How, or the purpose for which, you will use the personal data that you are processing.
- Identification and assessment of risks to individuals.
- Any measures you will take to minimize and prevent risk to the individuals involved.

And a DPIA should assess factors like:

- Is personal data processing necessary and proportionate to meet your goals?
- Are the risks involved worth the desired outcomes?
- Is there a need to contact a supervising authority?

After the DPIA is complete and before processing begins:

- Assess if there is still a high risk to individuals after mitigation and weigh the severity of any impact on individuals.
- Publish the DPIA with sensitive information redacted.
- Integrate the results of the DPIA into the project plan.
- Track and monitor the project against the DPIA to maintain privacy.

Some examples of events that would require a DPIA before processing begins include:

- A bus system implementing onboard cameras to monitor passengers and drivers.
- An HR department planning to use a new system to process employee records.

- A corporation using biometric data for access control.
- A crypto wallet application collecting personal information to verify user identities.
- A genealogy organization collecting and processing genetic data.
- A marketing firm deploying a machine-learning algorithm to personalize triggered emails.[151]

In contrast, there are scenarios that probably don't require a DPIA. For example, you likely would not need one if you've already performed a DPIA on a product offered in the EU and you are adding new features that do not process personal information in a new or different way.

Ultimately, how easily you can conduct DPIAs depends entirely on your data map. Keep DPIA requirements in mind when building your data map so that you can easily address DPIA parameters on processes you already have in place. And once those parameters become a core part of how your organization processes data, you'll be on a clear path to achieve privacy by design for any new products, processes, and features you launch.

What to Look for in Data-Mapping Tools

In theory, data mapping can be done manually. In practice, it's not recommended. Unless you're a very small company and processing the data of only a handful of users, the process will be extremely challenging. By the time you finish mapping everything, there's a high chance your organization will have new data sources to map. Data-mapping tools can also help with other requirements, such as populating RoPAs. Finding the right data-mapping software will require some careful planning and analysis. Here's what to look for:

1. **Ease of Use and Flexibility.** Data mapping can be challenging enough on its own. The software you choose shouldn't make your job harder. There will be a learning curve, but your data-mapping tool should be as user-friendly as possible so that even those who aren't used to such software can master it quickly. Flexibility is also key. Each business and each data-privacy regulation has its particularities, so you need room to customize the process.

   Also check the data visualization options. This is not mandatory, but it will make your life a lot easier. Imagine trying to view your data map, looking for patterns, and trying to explain security measures without a simple and clear visualization option. It's possible, but it won't be easy. A data flow diagram will simplify this step a lot.

2. **Mapping Capabilities.** When selecting a data-mapping tool, you'll need to make sure it can support all the types of data you work with and all the formats in which you store it. This can include databases, spreadsheets, and other file formats. Without the right mapping capabilities, you'll be unable to capture all the details needed, including relationships between sets of data or storage units. Most data-privacy-mapping software is ready for this, but you might still find the occasional tool that is built for non–data privacy purposes capable of mapping your data.

3. **Security and Compliance.** If you want to be compliant, ensure the tool you use for data mapping is also compliant. Find out what security measures it has in place and how it handles sensitive data. The last thing you want is to insert a vulnerability into your system by using a noncompliant tool.

4. **Collaboration and Integration Capabilities.** Data mapping is often a team effort, so it's best to choose a tool that has collaboration features. Preferably, select one that allows multiple people to work on the project simultaneously. Tracking changes and the option to leave comments will also come in useful for large teams.

   Your data-mapping solution will also need to integrate with your other systems. Check for compatibility and other integration options. Can this software work with your other data management tools? Don't forget about technical support. No matter how good your team is, it's always best to know the new software comes with support in case you run into any difficulties.

5. **Vendor Monitoring.** As I mentioned earlier, it's ultimately your responsibility to vet how vendors treat (and pass on) the data you've collected. Additionally, vendors frequently make changes to their policies, whether because of shifting imperatives or in response to new regulations. It would take a full-time, dedicated worker to manually touch base with each vendor associated with your business to check on these changes. Software solutions that can alert you to those changes can be the difference between high- and low-risk partnerships. We'll take a deeper dive into vendor risk in Chapter 10.

Compliance Deep Dive

By the time you've completed data mapping, you'll have a deep understanding of what data your organization processes and what it does with that data. Your compliance first look gave you a broad sense of the regulations that apply to you. Now that you understand all of your company's data practices, it's important to confirm whether you're obligated to comply with any other privacy laws and then figure out what further actions you may need to take to be compliant. For example, did you discover that your restaurant group in the Pacific Northwest processes data from folks in Colorado, Connecticut, and the United Kingdom when they sign up for your email newsletter? Turns out, you need to comply with regulations from those respective regions. While every privacy law aims to protect consumer data, they all go about it differently, so it's important to understand the nuances among different laws. This is where working with a privacy expert and/or appointing a DPO (even if you're not legally obligated to) will be a huge help in ensuring your compliance.

Your compliance deep dive is when you aim to leave no stone unturned when determining your organization's legal obligations across all privacy laws. Having a structured system in place for your RoPAs and DPIAs is a great start—but there is more to compliance. As you figure out your remaining obligations, walk through these key areas.

Determine what disclosures you need to make. Each privacy law has its own disclosure requirements, so it's important to understand the nuances of each one that applies to your organization. For example, before a business collects any personal information, the CPRA requires them to:

- Share the categories of personal information collected about consumers.
- Explain why they use the categories of information.
- Include a "do not sell/share" link if the business sells or shares personal data.
- Link to their privacy policy, which must include consumers' privacy rights and information on how to exercise them.

The GDPR requires businesses to share a privacy notice in a "concise, transparent, intelligible, and easily accessible form." The privacy notice should include:

- Why your organization processes personal data, including a legal basis.
- The third-party recipients, or categories of recipients, who will receive personal data.
- Whether you transfer data to a different country and, if so, how it's protected.
- The amount of time data is stored or the criteria used to determine when to delete data.
- Data-subject rights, including the right to withdraw consent and lodge a complaint with a supervisory authority.
- Whether you use an automated decision-making system, why it's used, and the consequences of its use.
- The identity and contact information for the organization, its representative, and the data-protection officer.
- Whether sharing personal data is required and the consequences of failing to provide it.

If your business obtains data indirectly, you don't need to include the last bullet point. However, you must disclose all of the categories of data collected.

Remember: Each law has its own disclosure requirements, so make sure to review the text of the relevant law or laws you identified as being applicable to your organization. What's more, you have to actually act on what you say in your privacy policy.

Implement the right contracts. Contracts ensure that everyone you do business with understands their data-privacy requirements, so make sure you have the proper contracts in place. This will protect your business and your customers' personal data by holding everyone you work with to the standards established by data-protection laws.

Under California regulations, you'll need to have contracts in place with relevant third-parties that are handling personal data, specifically service providers and contractors. The CPRA requires companies to have a contract with service providers and contractors that:

- Specifies that personal data is shared or sold for limited and specific purposes.
- Requires the service provider or contractor to comply with CPRA regulations.
- Gives the business permission to take steps to ensure the transfer of personal information is done according to CPRA requirements.
- Requires the service provider or contractor to notify the business if they are unable to meet CPRA obligations.
- Authorizes the business to take action to stop and rectify any unauthorized use of personal data.

If a business carries out service provider or contractor transfers, it should also ensure transfers meet the requirement for "business purposes" and prohibit the service provider or contractor from:

- Selling or sharing personal data.
- Retaining, using, or disclosing personal information for nonbusiness purposes.
- Retaining, using, or disclosing personal information outside the scope of the business relationship between the business and service provider or contractor.

Pay special attention to whether you share data across borders. You'll uncover this in data mapping, and it's a critical detail when it comes to contracts. Put simply, if data is crossing borders, it's essential to know where it's going and what contracts you're using to get it there. If you realize you're transferring data without a legal agreement, it might be time to decide where to store that data.

After a data-mapping exercise, some companies will decide to move the data to a storage center elsewhere. Suppose you can't legally transfer the data overseas. In that case, it's likely possible to store the data in a cloud located in the same jurisdiction as data subjects about whom you've collected data.

Establish how you're handling incoming SRRs. Almost all of the major privacy laws, including all of the state laws implemented in the last few years, contain requirements for handling SRRs.

When a person (or "data subject") submits an SRR—for any reason or no reason at all—your organization is required to respond with a copy of any information you have on the subject. Subjects can typically request the following:

- Confirmation that you process their personal information.
- Access to the personal data you have about them.
- Your legal basis for processing their data.
- The amount of time you will store their data (or the criteria you'll use to determine that period—i.e., "as long as you're a customer").
- Any relevant information about automated decision-making and profiling.
- Any relevant information about how your organization obtained the data.
- The names of any third parties who will receive a copy of their personal information.

If you don't respond within thirty or forty-five days (depending on the applicable law), your organization may face significant regulatory fines or penalties. There is no "right" way to respond to an SRR, but your company should have a plan to handle them when you receive one. You'll be well on your way to being able to respond to SRRs easily after you complete data mapping. If you use software to help with these tasks, it will likely have built-in capabilities to help with SRR responses. Chapter 9 will walk you through best practices for managing SRRs.

Ensure engineering is following privacy-by-design principles. While a data-protection officer may be the ringleader of your privacy protocols, every department should do its part to adhere to data-privacy regulations. A big part of that is privacy by design, which we touched on earlier. Privacy by design is an engineering principle that emphasizes implementing privacy into your products from the beginning. And it's more than just a good idea. Article 25 of the GDPR speaks specifically to data protection by design, saying that "the controller shall, both at the time of the determination of the means for processing and at the time of the processing itself, implement appropriate technical and organizational measures."[152] According to the seven foundational principles of privacy by design, businesses should create a system that is:

- Proactive, not reactive.
- Designed with privacy as the default setting.
- Developed with embedded privacy features.
- A win-win approach with no unnecessary trade-offs for full functionality.
- Protective of the full life cycle of data with end-to-end encryption.
- Marked by visibility and transparency.
- User-centric.

Privacy by design may require you to eventually redesign some of your company's longstanding products or features. As you create new ones, start with privacy in mind to reduce your workload later and ensure compliance from the very start.

Perform due diligence and ongoing vendor monitoring. You may run the most compliant business in the world, but a noncompliant vendor could ruin your credibility. That's why vendor risk monitoring is so important.

Checking your vendors' privacy practices when you hire them isn't enough. Continual monitoring is essential. Doing this yourself is challenging and time-consuming, but you can use software solutions to automate tasks like:

- Assigning a privacy rating to vendors according to their privacy practices.
- Notifying you of changes in privacy ratings.
- Tracking data to fourth and fifth parties.
- Alerting you to vendor lawsuits that could put the vendor out of business or create a risk for your company.

As you monitor your privacy practices, check in on your vendors too. You're responsible for the data you collect—even once it's delivered to a third party.

Incorporate feedback. A feedback loop will help your organization continuously improve its privacy program. If you or other team members discover risks—and it's normal to find a few—don't keep that information to yourself. Communicate your results immediately so you can make updates as soon as possible.

Data Minimization: Why Less Is More

Remember the '90s and aughts? You may recall from Chapter 2 that they were a sort of Wild West for the data world. With no laws to regulate how data was handled, many companies grabbed all the information that they could about site visitors with the hopes of monetizing it someday. It didn't matter if the data wasn't necessary for them to do their work. They took what they could because . . . why not?

As we know, that all changed when the GDPR entered the scene. The GDPR revolutionized the data-privacy world, setting the framework for businesses to create strategies to protect personal data. The regulation introduced seven principles of data protection, which we covered in Chapter 5. They are:

- Lawfulness, fairness, and transparency.
- Purpose limitation.
- Data minimization.
- Accuracy.
- Storage limitation.
- Integrity and confidentiality (security).
- Accountability.

If you're doing business with residents or citizens of the EU, you must implement all seven principles into your data-privacy strategy.

As we wrap up our coverage of the Compliance, Audit & Review pillar of your privacy program, it's a good time to zero in on the third principle—data minimization—since it has such a huge effect on the data you collect and process. And the GDPR isn't alone in requiring data minimization; the CPRA includes it too.

Article 5(1)(c) of the GDPR defines data minimization by saying that personal data should be "adequate, relevant and limited to what is necessary in relation to the purposes for which they are processed."[153] In other words, businesses should only collect essential information and only keep it as long as it's actually needed. The GDPR doesn't define "adequate, relevant, and limited," but it does require that the information be "necessary" for processing. If your business holds information it doesn't use for processing, you need to assess the data you collect and how you use it.

When it comes to data, some businesses still save everything. Like a bad episode of *Hoarders*, personal and nonpersonal data can be found scattered across systems, never to be processed. This is a bad idea, and the reasons go beyond compliance. Sure, the GDPR and CPRA require data minimization. But its benefits also include:

- **Saving money by reducing data storage.** Collecting data is expensive. Your business incurs the cost of data storage, collection, analysis, and maintenance.
- **Reducing your ecological impact by saving energy.** Aside from the dollar amount, storing and processing data requires energy. Cut costs and energy usage by culling all unnecessary data.
- **Increasing processing speed.** As a bonus, your processing speed will improve, and the time needed to process data will decrease.
- **Limiting consequences in case of data loss or breach.** Imagine getting fined for a data breach that includes information you never needed in the first place. Limiting the data you retain on customers can reduce your financial liability if a breach occurs.
- **Building trust with customers.** Data minimization goes a long way in building brand trust.

Compliance with the data minimization principle takes time, but it's worth the effort. Here are steps you can take to get there and reduce your risk:

- Determine the "adequate, relevant, and necessary" data to collect from customers, and only collect what is necessary.
- Know who uses the data and for what purposes.
- Only use the data for necessary purposes.
- Only share data when necessary and share the least

amount of information possible.

- Understand where the data is stored.
- Always get consent when collecting data. More on consent in the next chapter.
- Make it easy for customers to access, modify, or delete their data. We'll show you how to do that in the next chapter too.
- Delete data when it's no longer necessary for processing.

TL;DR CHEAT SHEET

- This pillar of your privacy program helps you process and organize the data you collect while staying aware of relevant laws and regulations.
- The three steps you must take are a compliance first look, data mapping, and a compliance deep dive.
- A compliance first look helps you determine the major privacy laws that apply to your organization.
- Data mapping identifies and organizes all the data your company collects and stores, including the source, flow, and destination. You can do data mapping manually, but we recommend using a data mapping tool (pay attention to ease of use, flexibility, capabilities, security, compliance, collaboration and integration capacity, and vendor monitoring).
- A compliance deep dive focuses on your specific requirements to set up systems for essentials such as disclosures, contracts, SRRs, and vendor monitoring.
- Fulfill your record of processing activities (RoPA) requirements, which is a snapshot of all your data processing practices in a single document.
- Execute your data protection impact assessments (DPIAs) for every major project, new feature rollout, or additional product or service that requires processing PI.
- Practice data minimization by only collecting adequate, relevant, and limited data. This will also save money by reducing data storage costs, minimize your ecological impact by saving energy, increase processing speed, limit consequences in case of data loss or breach, and build trust with customers.

CHAPTER 9

Notice, Consent & Choice

So far, much of what we've covered about building a privacy program has focused on your company's internal systems. **Governance & Accountability** ensures you have a great team and governing framework in place, and **Compliance, Audit & Review** gives you clarity on what data you handle and what you do with it.

Those pillars are essential for getting your preliminary privacy ducks in a row, especially on an organizational level. **Notice, Consent & Choice** takes a deeper dive into the public-facing side of your privacy program. You know all those people whose data you hope to collect and process? Privacy laws grant those folks data-subject rights that require you to communicate your plans with them. And each data subject needs to confirm they're okay with your plans before you touch their data. They also have the right to ask what data of theirs you have, find out how you're using it, and request that you stop at any time—among other rights. I introduced data-subject rights earlier, so they're no surprise. The Notice, Consent & Choice pillar of your privacy program helps you adopt best practices for addressing those rights.

I mentioned in Chapter 5 that many privacy laws follow a notice and consent model. This means their core focus is on how organizations notify data subjects of their personal data practices and how data subjects give consent to use their personal data. Notice, Consent & Choice covers all of that ground. In other words, your practices in this area are a big deal. Not only are there lots of rules to follow, but your practices are visible to regulators, making them an easy target for enforcement authorities to scrutinize. Your practices here also offer some of the biggest opportunities to build—or lose—trust with people who interact with your company.

Everything in this pillar falls into three categories:

- **Notices:** Notifying your consumers about what data you collect, why you collect it, and what you do with it is essential. It's both compliant with data-privacy regulation and the right thing to do. You'll achieve this through your privacy policy, cookie policy, and any other notices and disclosures that may be required in your industry. These notices need to be accurate, up to date, and kept in compliance with new and changing data-privacy laws.

- **Consent Management:** This is your system for obtaining, managing, and documenting consent from individuals to collect, use, and share their personal information—and it's a key component of both privacy ethics and regulatory compliance. Consent requirements vary among different jurisdictions, so your consent-management system needs to be nimble enough to adapt and comply with a data subject's local laws. Variations include whether consent must be opt in, opt out, and/or include specific language or consent controls. Most of this will be achieved through cookie banners, though consumers can also opt out via SRR or by using a universal opt-out signal like the Global Privacy Control. You'll also need a system for operationalizing data subject consent preferences and proving and recording consent preferences without violating privacy.

- **Subject Rights Request Management:** You're already familiar with SRRs—that is, data-subject access requests. Organizations need a system in place to receive, process, and respond to requests from data subjects who choose to exercise their data-privacy rights. SRRs can be one of the most visible aspects of your organization's data-privacy operations. Consumers won't always be aware of what work you do on a day-to-day basis, but they will notice if your privacy program is unable to meet their request within required timeframes or if your response contains errors.

The rest of this chapter unpacks these three categories so that you're armed with best practices for communicating and interacting with data subjects about their rights.

Notice: Say What You Do and Do What You Say

Notice sounds simple, right? Just tell people what you plan to do, then do it. And it is simple . . . sort of. The challenge is that you're trying to articulate all of your data practices—which are multilayered and complex—in an easy-to-read document that doesn't sound like a bunch of legal jargon. And let's face it: most privacy statements do read like legal jargon, which is not a good move. Not only do the GDPR and CPRA require you to use clear, transparent language in your privacy policies, but doing so is a simple way to build trust with anyone who interacts with your company.

Most organizations have two key privacy notices: their **privacy policy** and their **cookie policy**. It's okay to build on templates for these policies as long as you put in the work to significantly customize them so they accurately represent your company's practices. As we covered in Chapter 7, your privacy policy doubles as your program's governing framework. Yes, it tells the public what you do, but it also tells *you* what you do. There's a lot going on in any organization's privacy program, so it's important to have one accurate and thorough ruling document to refer back to.

There's a lot of temptation to copy and paste other organizations' policies. This is a bad idea. Aside from the missed opportunity to clarify all of your organization's data-privacy practices, copying and pasting also puts your organization at risk of making false claims. In 2019, the FTC settled with five companies who falsely claimed self-certification under the Privacy Shield, a framework that allowed companies to transfer data from EU countries to the United States in a way that complied with the GDPR.[154] While the Court of Justice of the European Union (CJEU) has since invalidated the US-EU Privacy Shield, many organizations have retained the certification since it still shows a commitment to strong privacy principles. Making a false claim along these lines would be detrimental to a company's reputation, not to mention the legal mess it could cause.

Privacy notices are unique to each organization and are worth the time it takes to get them right. Cisco's 2022 consumer privacy survey revealed that a company's data-privacy practices, and particularly their privacy notices, play a huge role in shaping consumers' opinion of that company. Seventy-six percent of respondents said they wouldn't buy from a company if they didn't trust how the company handled their data.[155] When asked what they felt was the most important activity organizations can do to build trust with customers when it comes to their data, respondents' top-ranking action was to provide clear information on how their data is being used. In other words, if you're not forthright about your data-handling practices, building trust will be an uphill battle.

Let's take a closer look at the two key policies your company will need: a privacy policy and a cookie policy.

Privacy Policies

By now, you're familiar with the basics of what goes into a privacy policy. If you need a refresher, jump to the Privacy Policy Checklist on page 153. You're likely still developing some of the practices that you'll describe in your policy if you're creating your privacy program from scratch. As you build each element, aim to write an explanation of each one. That text will become a part of your privacy policy. This is easier said than done, no question. One of the greatest challenges of creating a privacy policy is trying to articulate how user data is treated in a way that makes simple sense to users and is still thorough enough to capture everything a company does with data *and* fulfill its legal obligations. This is often a reason people fall back on legal jargon. Hiding behind vague legal terms can feel like a catch-all that covers your bases, but that practice is probably not helping you as much as you might hope.

So, what to do? First, don't attempt to write your whole policy in a single sitting. Tackle writing an explanation of each part of your privacy program as you hone that element. If you or someone on your team can't describe each part of your program in simple terms, that may be a signal that you need to spend a bit more time streamlining your processes.

Also aim to get other departments involved. Remember all those folks you spoke with from other departments in your company when building out your Governance & Accountability pillar? Once you feel you have a solid draft of your policy, go back to those colleagues and ask them if the text that applies to their work is clear to them. Does it describe what they actually do with data? Do they do anything else with data that isn't mentioned in the policy?

Be sure to pull in various business groups that might not seem obvious. The IT team, the engineering team, and even the sales team all touch and use customer data at some point, so it makes sense that they would at best provide input on the policy or at least review a draft to ensure that what's being conveyed about company practices maps to how their departments use data.

The bottom line is to put in the work to fully understand all of your company's data practices. If you get the fundamentals wrong, your policy will fall short. Be as straightforward as you can in your descriptions of those practices and then ensure the rest of the organization doesn't deviate from those descriptions.

Cookie Policies

You're also pretty familiar with cookies by now and know that certain kinds are essential for websites to run efficiently. They collect user data and use that information to improve each user's experience on the site. This information can provide better content, personalized ads, and more.

All that efficiency is super useful, but it quickly becomes problematic under most data-protection laws. In some jurisdictions, you need to provide users with a means of opting out of cookie usage. In others, they need to opt in before you can load any nonessential cookies. And in most situations, you need proof of consent (jump to page 198 for more on this). These laws also require you to inform your users about what data you collect from them and how you use it, among other requirements. That's where your cookie policy comes in—and it's a vital part of compliance.

A cookie policy is a document containing a list of all the cookies used on a website, along with detailed information about each one. It also helps users understand how their data is used and how long the cookies will remain on their device. It's important to understand that a cookie policy is not the same as a privacy policy. Your privacy policy includes information about all the data you collect, process, store, or transfer. A cookie policy looks strictly at the cookies that track user data.

Many websites choose to include their cookie policy in their privacy policy. While that's not wrong, it can be confusing and create problems down the line. For instance, cookie policies are explicitly required by the EU ePrivacy Directive and the GDPR, and while they can be integrated into your privacy policy, it's safer to have an explicit, separate document you can point to.

A cookie policy is also not the same as a cookie banner, but the two go hand in hand. Your cookie policy gives all the details about what cookies you use, why you use them, and how. The banner is how you collect consent and is often a feature of your consent-management platform. We'll dig into cookie banners and consent-management platforms in a minute. For now, let's keep going with your cookie policy since, like your privacy policy, it captures all of your cookie practices.

If you use cookies on your website, you need a cookie policy. Strictly necessary first-party cookies are exempt from privacy laws and can load with or without the user's consent. Other cookies used to gather data for analytics, marketing (also known as advertising or targeting), and functionality (also known as personalization)—are more complicated and require informed consent. Your cookie policy is there to tell users what these cookies do so they can decide whether they're okay with that. Here are some things your policy should touch on:

- What types of cookies you use.
- What personal data the cookies process.
- Where in the world the personal data will be transferred to/processed.
- The purposes of these cookies.
- How long the cookies track users.
- How users can opt in or opt out of cookie usage.
- What users can do if they give their consent but then change their minds.

The policy should be available in all the languages in which a service is provided. If you have a multilingual website, you will need to translate the cookie policy in all those languages.

Your policy needs to be updated as often as your cookie practices change. Cookie providers may often change the types of cookies they upload or their filenames. Other teams with website access at your organization may implement a solution that uses cookies without letting your compliance or legal team know. Modern business websites are often subject to change frequently, so it can be easy to lose track of what sorts of cookies you've deployed.

To keep your policy up to date, you'll need to perform regular scans of your site to take a catalog of the cookies in use on your site and what functions they perform. This is where automation is your friend. Consent-management platforms can manage cookie consent on your site as well as scan and categorize the cookies you use. This is essential, since you can't block or permit cookies based on user consent if you don't know what cookies are on your site and what they're doing.

Cookie Policy Example

Let's look at a real cookie policy so you can see these principles in action. Osano's cookie policy (at osano.trusthub.com/cookies) begins with information on how cookies are used. It continues with ways to disable cookies and then details the different types of cookies used on Osano's website. Finally, it lists each cookie file, along with its source, purpose, and expiration date.

This is, more or less, what your cookie policy should contain. You may choose a slightly different structure. For instance, some prefer to list the cookie files before explaining what each type of cookie does. What matters is to make sure your policy contains all the necessary information and is easy to read even for less-experienced users.

And ultimately, disclosure is key. Whether or not a regulation specifies that a cookie policy is necessary, all data-privacy laws feature some language about the importance of disclosing your data practices to your users. When in doubt, err on the side of transparency. You need to inform users of what cookies you use, their purposes, sources, and expiration date. It's good for building trust and for keeping the compliance police away.

Consent: No Cookies
for You (Until You Get Permission)

Cookie policies and privacy policies both fall into a sort of chicken-or-egg conundrum. Which comes first? Developing the policy, or developing the practice? The answer is both. If you're building a privacy program from scratch, your policies and practices will grow in tandem—and then keep developing together. I mentioned this when I covered privacy policies. The *how* behind creating the practices that you'll explain in your privacy policy spans all of the chapters in this book's Part 2. Here, we'll dig into the *how* behind creating the cookie practices you'll explain in your cookie policy.

It's so important to get cookies right since they're such a common method of user-data collection and a major source of risk. When investigating a business, regulators will often look for cookie compliance first since their use is so widespread. Fortunately, becoming cookie compliant is straightforward, even if it's not necessarily easy.

Let's start with an overview of cookie compliance requirements. Each privacy law comes with its own particularities regarding cookies, but cookie compliance primarily starts with the **notice** piece we've covered so far. You need to inform users you use cookies and explain how and why you use them. You'll achieve that in your cookie policy. The other piece of cookie compliance is **consent management**. At its most basic level, consent management is your method for informing users about how your business collects and uses data and giving them the opportunity to consent or refuse such use. You also need to keep records of each user's consent preferences and proof that you acted on their consent.

Privacy laws like the GDPR and the CPRA require the visitor's consent and proof of consent each time you process their personal data. For cookie usage, this translates into a few steps beyond having a cookie policy. You need:

- To inform visitors you're using cookies and give them the option to accept or not. Depending on the law, it may even be illegal to load nonessential cookies until the visitor gives consent.
- A backend that captures consent records for auditing.
- The ability to block cookies that are not consented to.
- A way to categorize cookies.
- A preference center that enables visitors to update, add, and revoke their consent.

- The ability to show different language, preference, and consent options based on the local law.

Cookie banners are a common way to quickly and unobtrusively meet all of these requirements. We've all encountered cookie banners as website users. A cookie banner is a pop-up that appears when you visit a website for the first time, informing you about the use of cookies, asking for your consent, or both. And they're a core component of consent management.

The Different Types of Cookie Banners and Consent

There are three primary types of cookie banners: **notice only**, **opt in**, and **opt out**. While there are variations within each type, these broadly represent the general approaches to obtaining user consent for the use of cookies on a website. I'll give examples of each of these later on; for now, let's focus on the kind of cookie banner text, information, and functionality you can expect to see on these variations.

1. **Notice-Only Cookie Banners.** A notice-only cookie banner, also known as an information-only banner, is a minimalistic approach that simply informs users about the website's use of cookies. It typically displays a brief message or notification at the bottom or top of the web page, alerting visitors to the presence of cookies and providing a link to the website's cookie policy. This type of banner does not seek explicit consent from users to place cookies on their devices but serves as a disclosure mechanism. While notice-only banners may be used in certain jurisdictions, they may not fully comply with the stricter requirements of modern data-privacy laws. They

don't live up to the GDPR's standards, for example. You can use them under the CPRA, but you'll also need certain links on your homepage to be compliant (more on that shortly).

2. **Opt-In Cookie Banners.** An opt-in cookie banner requires users to actively provide consent for the use of cookies. When users visit a website with an opt-in banner, they are presented with a clear message that explains the purpose of the cookies and their implications. Users are given the option to either accept or decline the use of cookies through an affirmative action, such as clicking an "Accept" or "Allow" button. Opt-in banners prioritize user control and align with the GDPR's principles of privacy by default. They require explicit consent from users before any cookies are placed on their devices.

3. **Opt-Out Cookie Banners.** In contrast to opt-in banners, opt-out cookie banners work on the premise that users are presumed to have given their consent unless they actively choose to opt out. These banners display a message that informs users about the website's use of cookies and provides them with the ability to manage their cookie preferences. This is key—if the user hasn't been informed about the use of cookies and isn't given a clear way to opt out, it's not a compliant opt-out banner. Often cookie banners that comply with US privacy laws take an opt-out approach.

GDPR Cookie Banner Examples

The GDPR doesn't explicitly mention cookies, but it does have several requirements for consenting to data processing and collection. The most important thing for website owners to know is how the GDPRdefines "consent." "Consent" of the data subject "means any freely given, specific, informed, and unambiguous indication of the data subject's wishes by which he or she, by a statement or by a clear affirmative action, signifies agreement to the processing of personal data relating to him or her."[156] So a GDPR-compliant cookie banner must:

- Not coerce or manipulate the user into giving consent—consent must be "freely given."
- Clearly describe what kind of data your website will collect upon consent and what the implications of giving consent are—that is, consent must be "specific, informed, and unambiguous."
- Prevent data collection from happening unless the user gives their consent first through an "affirmative action"—like clicking "Agree." That's what makes GDPR banners opt in.

Furthermore, because different cookies can be used for different purposes (such as marketing, analytics, and personalization), the GDPR requires that you give users granular control over the types of cookies they consent to or not. A user might be comfortable with analytics cookies that merely help diagnose site performance but not want cookies used for marketing purposes. An example cookie banner that meets these requirements looks like this:

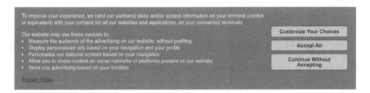

Specifically, this cookie banner complies with the French CNIL's requirements for GDPR compliance. As you can see, it:

- Clearly describes what it means to consent.
- Lists what you would be consenting to.
- Lists what the cookies will be used for.
- Links to a privacy policy.
- Allows users to select which categories of cookies they consent to.
- Allows users to reject cookies outright.

Here's another GDPR-compliant banner from France in the original French:

Note that both of these banners are compliant with the French CNIL's GDPR guidance even though they look a little different—one is vertically aligned and would appear on the side of the screen, while the other is horizontally aligned and would appear at the top; and the language they use is different.

If you were to cater to French citizens, you would obviously default to using the French language. But your cookie banner ought to adjust to the language preferences set by the individual user in their browser—that ensures the user is truly informed (as required by the GDPR).

Pour améliorer votre expérience, nous (et nos partenaires) stockons et/ou accédons à des informations sur votre terminal (cookie ou équivalent) avec votre accord pour tous nos sites et applications, sur vos terminaux connectés.

Notre site Web peut utiliser ces cookies pour :
- Mesurer l'audience de la publicité sur notre site, sans profilage
- Afficher des publicités personnalisées basées sur votre navigation et votre profil
- Personnaliser notre contenu éditorial en fonction de votre navigation
- Vous permettre de partager du contenu sur les réseaux sociaux ou les plateformes présents sur notre site Internet

Politique de confidentialité

Personnalisez vos choix

Accepter tout

Continuer sans accepter

The GDPR permits you to use different color schemes, styling, and placement of your cookie banner. But remember: consent must be "freely given" through an "affirmative action." So certain design practices that manipulate users into giving consent are forbidden by the GDPR. If you were to color the "Continue without Accepting" button the same shade as the background and thereby make the "Accept All" button easier to click, that would constitute a violation of the GDPR. Similarly, if your banner were incredibly small and appeared in a tiny corner of the screen, that would also violate the law.

One last important point to note about GDPR cookie banner examples: You may have noticed we referred to the CNIL's interpretation of the GDPR above. Each member state in the EU has its own data protection authority (DPA), and each DPA has its own interpretation of the GDPR. *That means each GDPR jurisdiction may require its own banner.* For example, take a look at this example of a GDPR-compliant banner that would display in Spain (again, translated into English):

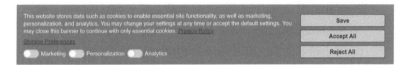

Rather than require a user to click a "Customize Your Choices" button as was the case with the French banner, the Spanish banner provides those choices right up front. The cookie banner's text is also different—these are all individual differences determined by the given jurisdiction's DPA.

Obviously, this makes providing a GDPR-compliant banner really difficult. To deploy a homegrown cookie consent banner solution, you'd have to research every DPA's interpretation of the GDPR and translate that interpretation into a compliant design. That's not to mention the difficulty of actually operationalizing all of this! Getting a GDPR-compliant cookie banner isn't just about finding the right examples of cookie banner text; the banner has to actually do what it says it will.

CPRA Cookie Consent Banner Examples

Like under the rules of the GDPR, your cookie banner's design will depend on the CPRA's specific requirements around consent and data collection. Here's a lightly edited passage that presents what the CPRA has to say about cookie consent:

A business that sells or shares consumers' personal information or uses or discloses consumers' sensitive personal information [. . .] shall:

- Provide a clear and conspicuous link on the business's internet homepages, titled "Do Not Sell or Share My Personal Information," to an internet web page that enables a consumer [. . .] to opt out of the sale or sharing of the consumer's personal information.
- Provide a clear and conspicuous link on the business's internet homepages, titled "Limit the Use of My Sensitive Personal Information," that enables a consumer [. . .] to limit the use or disclosure of the consumer's sensitive personal information.

I cleaned up the text for clarity and ease of reading (surprisingly, legal texts can be a bit convoluted), but if you want to take a look at the original, the relevant passage in the CPRA is Section 1798.135.[157]

You'll notice that this section of the CPRA doesn't mention anything about banners—the CPRA actually doesn't require businesses to include links titled "Do Not Sell or Share My Personal Information" or "Limit the Use of My Sensitive Personal Information" on their banner; merely that they appear on the "business's internet homepages." Thus, a CPRA-compliant cookie consent banner might look like this:

This website stores data such as cookies to enable essential site functionality, as well as marketing, personalization, and analytics. By remaining on this website you indicate your consent. Cookie Policy.

This banner conforms with the CPRA's requirement to provide notice, as stated in Section 1798.100: "A business that controls the collection of a consumer's personal information shall, at or before the point of collection, inform consumers [regarding the personal information to be collected]."[158] It provides a link to a cookie policy, which contains further information required for CPRA compliance.

To be compliant, a business would also need to include the links mentioned above somewhere on their website homepage, usually in the footer.

The following is an example of a CPRA-compliant cookie consent banner that relies on opt-in consent; you won't collect any personal information from consumers unless they click "Accept" first.

Both of these banners comply with the CPRA—just note that you still need links titled "Do Not Sell or Share My Personal Information" or "Limit the Use of My Sensitive Personal Information" on your homepage.

How to Get Cookie Compliant

You're well on your way to understanding cookie compliance once you've become familiar with cookie policies and consent management. Now let's put all the pieces together. While sometimes challenging, the compliance journey is straightforward. Here are the steps:

1. **Start with a cookie audit and make a list of all the cookies you use.** First-party and third-party cookies both count for compliance purposes. You can do this manually or with a software tool. Either way, your goal is to identify the cookies you're serving, investigate each cookie for potential compliance issues, and resolve any compliance problems.

2. **Choose a consent-management platform.** These are complete solutions that offer everything from cookie banners to tools for keeping records. Often, they support other data-privacy needs beyond just cookie consent management, like executing SRRs. Make sure your solution gets clear and informed consent from users. It should also be easy for them to read information about your use of cookies and revoke consent whenever they change their mind.

3. **Publish a cookie policy.** Be transparent and comprehensive. List all the cookies you use and their type, scope, and duration.

4. **Review your policy and conduct a new cookie audit.** You can't write a cookie policy once and then forget about it for all eternity. On the contrary, you should update your cookie policy every six to twelve months or whenever you start using new cookies or become subject to new laws.

5. **Stay up to date with privacy laws.** More and more

data-privacy laws are coming into effect. Just because you're compliant with everything that applies to you today doesn't mean you'll be compliant with new regulations as well. Keep an eye on new laws and on how they may affect your business. Working with a legal consultant will also help.

Top Challenges with Cookie Compliance

Cookie compliance is not a complicated process. But it comes with various challenges, some of which are easier to overcome and some harder. These are the difficulties we see folks encounter the most:

1. **Keeping records of consent.** The GDPR requires proof of consent, and the only way to do that is to record each user's choice. You need to know when a user gave their consent and for what cookies.

2. **Allowing users to revoke consent.** Someone agreed to cookies. Great! But what if they change their mind? The GDPR clearly states that data subjects have the right to withdraw consent. If you kept the records mentioned previously, you're one step closer to overcoming this challenge as well. But you need to make sure your consent-management tool allows you to respond quickly each time someone changes their mind about cookies.

3. **Correctly categorizing cookies.** Informed consent means you need to tell your users about all the cookie categories you use. But categorizing them correctly may prove to be more challenging than expected. A good consent-management platform will help you overcome this challenge quite easily, though.

4. **Balancing compliance and user experience.** Have
   you ever entered a website only to be deeply annoyed
   by a cookie banner that keeps getting in your way?
   Unfortunately, this is needed for opt-in consent—
   the banner needs to stay in place until the user clicks
   on it. Does that really mean you need to make it impossible to browse the site, though? It doesn't. As long
   as you don't assume consent, they should be able to browse
   the site with essential cookies only. But finding the right
   balance can be challenging.

Choice: Subject Rights Request Management

All of your work on notice and consent is grounded in one set of principles: data-subject rights. Remember those? We took a first look
at them in Chapter 4. They're the backbone of the GDPR, CPRA,
and most other data-privacy laws. Before we go further, here's a recap
of those rights. While the details in each law may differ a bit, these
themes are generally universal among key privacy laws:

- **Right to Know:** People have a right to know what personal data you retain that relates to them.
- **Right to Opt Out:** Most laws allow people to opt out of
  their personal data being used in a variety of ways, most
  commonly for the purposes of targeted advertising
  and the sharing or sale of their data.
- **Right to Access:** People have a right to get a copy
  of all the personal data you have about them.
- **Right to Correct:** People have a right to make sure
  the data you have about them is accurate and to correct
  it if it's not.
- **Right to Delete:** People have the right to request all their

personal data be removed. Many laws even require you to pass on the request to any third parties to whom you've sold the data or with whom you've shared it.

- **Right to Data Portability:** Many laws require you to provide personal data in a format that would allow people to take that data and provide it to another service provider.
- **Right to Nondiscrimination:** The CPRA in particular protects data subjects from discrimination for exercising their data-privacy rights.

Notice and consent cover the right to know and the right to opt out, but clearly there's more work to be done. The last five bullets in this list are associated with SRRs.

The term "SRR" first came about as an acronym for "subject rights request," but it's come to be shorthand for any time someone looks to exercise a privacy right. While you might be asked, "How do you handle SRRs?" or "What's your SRR solution?" the question your organization actually needs to answer is: "If someone chooses to exercise one of their data-privacy rights, do you know how to take in that request, process it appropriately, and fulfill it within the required timeframe?" You have to be able to answer this with a confident *yes* to be compliant with major privacy laws.

The rest of your Notice, Consent & Choice pillar focuses on creating a system so you can do just that.

The Basics of Creating an SRR Program

These are the essential functions your SRR program needs to cover:

Request Submission

You need to offer an easy way for people—customers, employees, business partners, and anyone else whose personal data you hold—to submit a request to exercise their rights. Most laws require that this be explained in your privacy policy and with multiple pathways for making contact.

Request Verification

You have to ensure the person making the request is the person who owns the data. If you provide one person's data to another person making a request in bad faith, that's a breach.

Remember: it's crucial you don't collect more personal information than is necessary as you are doing this. Generally, it's best to ensure the verification is proportionate to the data the subject is looking to access. If it's just basic consumer data, having them log into their account with you should be good enough. If it's more sensitive data, you might have two-factor authentication, where you send them a code to a phone number or email address. Doing something like requiring a photo ID should be only for the most sensitive data situations and when you have no other good options.

If you reject a request, it should be for a really good reason. Most laws have exemptions for nuisance requests, like someone filing an SRR multiple times a week, or when fulfilling the request would be especially onerous. However, if it's only burdensome because your systems aren't in proper order, that's not a good reason at all. If you reject a request, you must explain your reasoning to the data subject. Make sure an actual person is involved in reviewing the rejection—especially if you are using some kind of automation. An automated rejection could set off triggers with privacy regulators.

Many laws also allow an "authorized agent" to file SRRs on behalf of other people, in cases, for example, in which elderly or incapacitated people need help with managing their personal data. These requests should be scrutinized closely, as many observers feel they are ripe for fraud and abuse.

Request Acknowledgment

Once you've verified the person is who they say they are (or not), you need to reply that you have received the request and are working to fulfill it (or not, if they aren't who they say they are and aren't an authorized agent).

Find the Data

If you're like most companies, you have data in lots of places. How will you locate all the data about *this* Jane Smith and ensure it's not about *that* Jane Smith? You'll be in a strong position to be able to do it well after going through data discovery and data mapping.

Assign Responsibility

Who within your organization will fulfill the request once you've found the relevant data? This may be a single person in some instances, or it may be a team of folks from multiple departments.

Communicate the Results

How do you let the person making the request know it's been fulfilled? You might do so via a data file they download, a message saying a piece of data has been corrected, or a receipt for their deleted data.

Record the Interaction

It's essential to document that you have received and fulfilled the request, not only because you'll want to prove you did your job if a complaint is lodged, but also because many laws require you to report how many requests you've received, how long it took to fulfill the requests, and more. Remember: don't create a bunch of new personal data you'll need to manage when you keep your records. The process should involve as little personal data as possible. This minimal amount of personal data for recordkeeping may not be used for any other purpose.

Learn from Each Request

It's important to have some mechanism in place for continually learning and making your process more efficient. How does everyone involved contribute feedback and make things better?

Skipping any one of the above steps could put you in serious danger of being out of compliance with any number of privacy laws.

Your SRR Team

Having a process in place is great, but if there aren't any people tasked with overseeing and operating it, it won't do you much good. Here are the folks you'll generally need to have involved.

The Data Subject

Most significant and at the center of this process is the data subject—the person who owns the personal data. While this might seem obvious, organizations often seem to forget that this is a living, breathing person who requires the same kind of thoughtful customer service you would provide to anyone accessing your products or services. Keep them top of mind.

The Privacy Leader

Whether you have a chief privacy officer, a data-protection officer, a compliance manager, or a director of data protection, someone on your team needs to be ultimately responsible for the effectiveness of your overall privacy program. Ideally, this person reports to the highest people in your organization and has the appropriate budget and resources.

The Subject Rights Manager

This could be your privacy leader, but it could also be someone on the team tasked with SRRs specifically. Regardless, it's vital that someone "owns" SRRs and advocates for the continual improvement and support of the process internally.

The Subject Rights Assignees

For every database or other location in which personal data lives in your organization, there is someone who must access that database and be able to correct, delete, or retrieve the appropriate data. These people might have special access or privileges and may not be on the privacy team but, instead, may be on the IT, marketing, sales, or product development teams. You need to make sure they are plugged into your process appropriately.

Once you have created your process and identified the people involved, the flowchart for SRRs might look a lot like this:

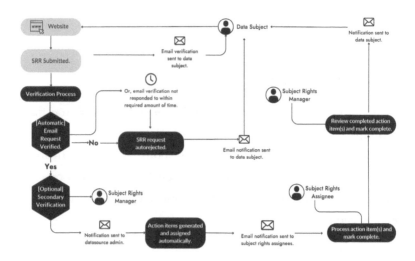

Developing Your SRR Policy

Whether you're starting from scratch or revamping an existing process, it's important to make sure you don't skip any steps as you adopt a new SRR fulfillment process.

One of the first things you need to do is develop an internal, written SRR policy. This is different from your privacy policy. Your SRR policy should outline your whole procedure, specifically mentioning how requests are handled from all the different possible constituencies: customers, employees, those with sensitive data, B2B partners, etc. A policy that treats every request the same is a bad policy, and a policy that doesn't outline the "how" and "who" of every step is a bad policy.

You'll need to make a lot of decisions when developing your policy. Here are the key topics you'll need to cover:

Will You Try to Apply Different Laws to Different Requests?

Is your program sophisticated enough to understand that California's law applies to this customer and the GDPR applies to that employee and therefore this SRR is due in forty-five days and this other one is due in thirty days? If not, you might want to treat all requests the same in terms of the rules that apply. Many organizations just figure out the strictest rules that apply to them globally and shape their policy around that.

Will You Apply Privacy Laws to Everyone?

Is your program sophisticated enough to understand that this customer is in Alabama and covered by no significant privacy law and this other person is in California and is covered by the CPRA? Many organizations just apply the same rules to everyone, as it can be challenging to know where a person is in the world when they interact with your organization.

Who Is Doing What?

It should say right in your policy who is responsible for each step. This ensures, too, that you update your policy any time you have significant turnover.

How Often Will You Review Your Policy?

An annual review is probably not often enough. You should have some kind of regular review process to make sure new laws or new people don't require a new bit of policy language.

How Will You Incorporate Feedback?

You should have a process for taking in feedback from all the stakeholders—data subjects, program managers, subject rights assignees, etc. If you intend to continually improve, how do you evaluate which ideas should be incorporated and which are frivolous or counterproductive? Many complaints to regulators result from frustrated and angry customers upset about the SRR process. If you have a history of ignoring feedback, regulators will likely look unkindly at that.

What's Your Data Retention Policy?

While this is part of your organization's larger privacy and data-protection policy, it's hugely necessary for SRR fulfillment. If you regularly get rid of data you no longer use or at least de-identify it, the SRR process will be much more streamlined and efficient. On the flip side, keeping data in databases that become outdated and clunky will make SRR fulfillment much more difficult. As just one example, many people don't consider the fact that company emails may contain employees' personal data. How long are you leaving those on the server?

Are You Updating Your Record of Processing Activity (RoPA) at the Same Time?

How you handle SRRs is often directly tied to your record of processing activity (RoPA). If you're processing data in a certain way, that will likely be reflected in the access report you produce. If your SRR policy and RoPA don't line up, something is amiss.

Who Else Needs to be Involved in Your SRR Process?

Once you've figured out the internal stakeholders for your process, look outward: Which vendors are you currently sharing data with? Who are you selling data to? Who is sharing data with you? Many laws confer onward obligations. For example, if someone requests you delete all the data you hold about them, California's privacy regime says you may have to pass that request along to anyone with whom you've shared the data unless an exemption applies. Can you actually pass that request along, and will they actually fulfill it?

Remember: just because a partner says they are doing something doesn't mean they are doing it. Figure out how to audit them in a respectful and collaborative way.

Your policy should be a living, breathing document that you constantly review for effectiveness and accuracy. If you want to set your team up for success, you need to make adjustments to your policy regularly.

Using Tools for Efficiency

While you may not need to answer all of the above questions or figure out every person who's going to be involved in your organization before purchasing software to help you, it's generally a good idea to do most of that work first. One of the biggest mistakes companies make is buying software products without an idea of how to deploy them effectively, making their policy and procedure a reflection of what they purchased and not necessarily a reflection of their company risk profile or values.

If you're feeling confident about your plans, though, or even as you start to get your plans in order, it is undoubtedly true that automating pieces of your process will help immeasurably in ensuring you are compliant in replying to SRRs. As you do your shopping, here are some things to consider:

Software shouldn't replace people entirely. Be suspicious of any company talking about removing your influence altogether. Privacy is a complex field, and context matters. One-hundred percent automation can mean giving up control over the process. It's good practice to keep checks and balances in place so a human is monitoring what's coming in and out of your tool and auditing how the tool is performing regularly.

You'll especially want to keep an eye on things like verification, denials, requests, or other places where you're potentially erecting barriers to people exercising their rights. Making a mistake there could have serious consequences. In 2021, for instance, the Austrian Post was fined a shocking €9.5 million for not allowing SRRs via email.[159]

Make sure you're tying in all of the places you store data. One of the most common mistakes companies make when automating their SRRs is failing to aggregate all the personal data they collect.

Automate what you can. With all of the above said, it's absolutely vital you automate those tasks that make sense. SRRs can be time-consuming, and if you can find a tool that can take in requests, acknowledge them, do basic validating, and reply to basic access requests, so much the better. Automating what you can allows you to point valuable people's time to those places where you genuinely need human oversight.

TL;DR CHEAT SHEET

- Notices tell your consumers what data you collect, why, and what you do with it. Most organizations have two key privacy notices: their privacy policy and their cookie policy.
- We've covered privacy notices already. Cookie policies should include what types of cookies you use, what PI the cookies process, where the data will be transferred, the purpose of the cookies, how long they will track a user, and how to opt in or opt out.
- Consent management is your system for obtaining, managing, and documenting consent from individuals to collect, use, and share their PI.
- The most widespread consent management tools are cookie banners, which inform visitors you're using cookies and give them the opportunity to accept or reject the use of cookies when they're visiting a website.
- A thorough consent management system also includes a backend that captures consent records for auditing; the ability to block cookies that are not consented to; a way to categorize cookies; a preference center that enables visitors to update, add, and revoke consent; the ability to show different language preferences; and consent options based on local laws.
- Cookie banners can be notice only, opt in, and opt out.

(continued...)

- Subject rights request (SRR) management responds to your data subjects' choices regarding what kind of information they allow you to collect and store and how.
- The basics of SRR management require you to offer an easy way to submit an SRR, verify each request, acknowledge the request, find the requested data, assign responsibility within your company, communicate the results, and record the interaction.

CHAPTER 10

Risk, Response & Resilience

D ata privacy would be a lot easier to manage if companies didn't share data outside their organizations. But in practice, that's nearly impossible. Every company, no matter its size, works with third parties to help it operate more efficiently. That usually requires it to share data on some level, whether it's personal employee information going to a health insurance provider or audience data being shared with a marketing firm. And unfortunately, all that sharing can expose organizations to a host of risks. That's why **Risk, Response & Resilience** is a critical pillar of your data-privacy program. Exposure to risk is a normal part of doing business. How you minimize that risk, respond when you encounter a problem, and work to stay resilient in the face of risk is what sets you apart as a trusted brand.

Sharing data with certain vendors will expose you to more risk than sharing with others. For example, a company that handles your organization's social media may not be as big of a risk as a vendor that processes payroll, simply because of the types of information they each need to access to provide their service. But even when risk is low, it's there—and it comes in many forms, including:

- **Cybersecurity risk:** Security breaches can disrupt your business's IT systems and leave you open to data loss.
- **Legal risk:** If your vendors aren't following applicable regulations, your company could be held liable, particularly in highly regulated markets like financial services, health care, and government organizations.
- **Privacy risk:** While privacy risk overlaps with legal risk, it's not a one-to-one match. Your vendors might violate data-privacy regulations and put you at legal risk, but they might also fail to meet your internal standards for consumer privacy. That could damage your brand and operations.
- **Reputational risk:** When a company suffers a security incident, either directly or through a vendor, its reputation takes a hit. Poor public perception could lead to reduced revenue, loss of customers, and more.
- **Financial risk:** A vendor could put your company in financial peril by causing issues with the supply chain, overspending, or by impacting revenue-generating activities.
- **Operational risk:** Depending on how critical the vendor is to your company, a vendor's ability to complete services as promised could have a direct impact on your organization's operations.

The big challenge with all types of risk exposure is that, so often, trouble starts due to actions that didn't even happen in your company. Our research shows that the average company shares its data with 730 different vendors, and third-party vendors are responsible for two out of every three data breaches.[160] Add to this the fact that your vendors also rely on third parties, and so on. Referred to as Nth parties, your vendors' vendors, services, applications, and IT infrastructures also put your organization at risk for a serious security incident. Yet only 15 percent of companies have an inventory of these downstream vendors.[161] Unfortunately, it's difficult to get this information. Short of using a software tool that has the capability to discover your vendors' Nth parties, the only option is to send questionnaires to your vendors asking them for this information. But this is slow and unreliable.

Even with robust contracts in place, a company ultimately can't control what a third party does with the data it shares—however it can be held accountable if a vendor mishandles that data. Organizations find themselves in this predicament all the time. In 2019, Quest Diagnostics faced several class action lawsuits after one of their vendors, a medical billing collection company, exposed the health information of nearly twelve million Quest Diagnostics patients.[162] That's one of many, many examples. The average cost of a data breach in the United States in 2023 was $9.48 million ($4.45 million global average), according to a report released by IBM.[163] Sixty percent of small businesses that suffer a cyberattack are unable to withstand the impact and go out of business within six months, according to the National Cybersecurity Alliance.[164] They just can't recover from the costs associated with legal consequences, regulatory actions, reputational damage, revenue loss, and sometimes even paying cyberattackers' ransoms. And perhaps it's no surprise that companies with the least rigorous privacy practices are nearly twice as likely to suffer a data breach as companies with excellent data stewardship.[165]

Fortunately, there's a straightforward way to avoid all of this trouble. It's a process called **vendor risk management** (also sometimes referred to as **third-party risk management**, or **TPRM**). This is your company's approach to vetting vendors and third-party service providers before you engage them so you can understand their privacy practices and the risks associated with doing business with them. A strong vendor risk management program also continually monitors your vendors to make sure that they maintain good security and data-privacy practices and that they remain compliant with all regulations.

Vendor risk management is essential to complying with data-privacy laws. Most major regulations, including the GDPR and the CPRA, require organizations to practice it. While the details change slightly from one regulation to another, the big ones expect companies to assess whether their vendors take measures to protect data subjects' rights. They also want companies to monitor their vendors for data-privacy compliance over the course of their relationship together and address data-privacy handling in their vendor contracts. That means you may need to work closely with your legal and procurement teams to figure out whether any of your existing contracts need to be updated or renegotiated to include privacy-related language.

Vendor risk management also helps protect your company from legal liability if you get tangled in a third-party breach. This is a big deal since organizations are often held accountable for their downstream partners' actions. When a breach occurs and authorities evaluate whether to file criminal charges against a company, one of the key factors they look at is whether a company was working to effectively monitor its vendors.[166] If they discover that a company was not actively monitoring its third-party vendors for risk, they consider whether the incident could have been avoided if they had been. If it could have been avoided with better vendor risk management, enforcement authorities tend to be less lenient.

Once we check our compliance and legal boxes, vendor risk management still delivers by helping to create transparency and build trust. Practicing it shows your customers and employees that you take their privacy seriously, which has a ripple effect that builds trust and boosts your bottom line.

Vendor risk management covers so much ground that setting up a program can feel intimidating. This chapter walks you through the big picture so you can be familiar with the key aspects of setting up a solid program. It's important to understand, though, that the details of how you manage vendor risk will depend on factors unique to your company, including:

- **Which privacy laws and regulations apply to you.** Each one has its own guidelines for factors such as what kind of personal data you're allowed to share with third parties, requirements for assessing third-party risk, monitoring third-party data-security practices, and contract management, among other things. You'll need to work closely with your legal counsel and/or data-protection officer if you have one to discover the rules that apply to your organization.
- **What kinds of data you process.** While the broad strokes may look the same from company to company, your specific approach to vendor risk management will look different if you're a health care company processing customers' private health information compared to if you're, say, an event-planning company or restaurant.
- **The types of vendors and third-party service providers you engage.** This goes hand in hand with the kind of data you process. If you're outsourcing tasks to vendors that require access to highly personal or sensitive information, your processes will adjust accordingly.
- **Buy-in across departments.** Interdepartmental collaboration plays a huge role in managing vendor risk. As much as you may try to centralize your vendors across departments, it's common for employees to engage new vendors and bypass your vendor onboarding process along the way. One study revealed that 80 percent of workers

admit to using SaaS applications at work without getting approval from IT.[167] There usually are no bad intentions at play—folks are just trying to make their jobs more efficient—but this can be a critical misstep from a privacy standpoint.

This last point highlights a key challenge: you can't truly manage vendor risk unless everyone in your company participates in the system you've set up. Your whole privacy program will be a cross-functional team sport, but vendor risk management is an element where full company buy-in is especially important, and one where you'll find the most naysayers and rule breakers. Part of your work here will be to regularly follow up with departments to make sure they're engaging with compliant vendors. But you need to do this carefully: this is a spot where a privacy professional will either be perceived as a blocker or as an enabler for everyone else in the company. Of course, you want the latter. Having a vendor risk management program that's easy to tap into will be a major help with this. Automate as much as you can and make the process of checking a vendor's privacy posture as simple as possible. If done well, your vendor risk management system will help you make huge strides in efficiency. If not, it can have the opposite effect—*and* make you more vulnerable to security and privacy risks along the way.

Making Your Company Risk Resistant

In a world where data sharing is unavoidable, your vendor risk management program is like a security system for keeping out vendors that don't comply with data-privacy regulations. Managing vendors requires a rigorous, ongoing look at your company's operations. To do that well, you'll start by setting up a system that streamlines your efforts. The core parts of that system are:

1. **Your accountability team.** This may be your data-privacy officer or someone else assigned to owning vendor risk management depending on what regulations require of your organization. It's also a good idea to have a point person who is accountable for vendor risk management in each department across the company.

2. **A control framework and risk methodology.** There is not a single control framework or risk methodology that's right for every organization, but every company should choose the one that best meets its needs. Two major entities that provide such standards are the National Institute of Standards and Technology (NIST) and the International Organization for Standardization (ISO). If you use software tools to manage your privacy program, they're usually built around the standards set by one or both of these organizations. If you're running your program manually, part of your work will be to research control frameworks and risk methodologies and work closely with a privacy expert to determine which are right for your company.

3. **A contract management system.** Every vendor relationship must start with a contract outlining the terms of your arrangement. If you haven't already, set up a system for managing contracts, keeping them up to date, and ensuring that each one includes any required language related to data-privacy practices. It may help to use a contract life cycle management tool to help automate much of this process. If you're a smaller company, it may work for you to manage contracts using a spreadsheet-driven system.

4. **Processes for vendor discovery, assessment, selection, onboarding, monitoring, and offboarding.** These processes are the backbone of your ongoing vendor risk management work. Once they're in place, you'll come

back to them again and again. Make sure you understand who on your accountability team is in charge
of each task, from due diligence to assessment questionnaires. Define how often you need to reassess vendors
and what the process looks like. If you're not sure what
a vendor assessment looks like, don't worry: there
are standard templates you can use to develop these
assessments. If you use privacy software tools, these templates may be integrated into the system. Also make
sure vendors understand your practices, along with when
and how to address potential risks and breaches.

5. **Automation tools.** If this all sounds complicated,
that's because it is—if you try to do it manually.
You can automate most of your vendor risk management
processes. Your automation needs will vary based on your
company's IT maturity and current processes. Make
sure to assess several tools to see how they can meet your
organization's specific needs. Here are a few questions
to consider when you're looking for an enterprise risk
monitoring platform:

- Does your organization have a current solution? If so,
  are there any features your compliance personnel wish
  it had or gaps that need to be addressed?
- How does the solution's automation work? Does
  it rely heavily on human input, or, once it's set up,
  can it run on its own? Can it perform tasks in bulk
  and alert your compliance officers of risks in real
  or near-real time?
- How comprehensive is the platform? Does it have capabilities that expand beyond onboarding and assessment,
  such as continuous monitoring?

- What happens if there's a breach and you have the vendor risk management solution in place?

Your vendor risk management program will run on these systems. Once they're up and running, your ongoing work will follow a predictable cycle that addresses **vendor discovery, assessment, selection, onboarding, monitoring**, and **offboarding**. Here's a closer look at each one:

Vendor discovery. This concept is simple: find out who your company's vendors are. In practice, it can be harder than it sounds depending on your company's size and complexity. You'll uncover a good amount of your vendors during data discovery and data mapping, but that's usually not enough. As I mentioned earlier, employees often engage new vendors without letting their legal or privacy teams know. You'll need to figure out whether your company has any of these unknowns. Then, make vendor discovery an ongoing part of your work so you can stay aware of any new vendors that join your company's ecosystem.

Once you've located a vendor, keep track of what data you share with it and for what purposes. You'll also need to make sure you address data sharing and handling as needed in your contract with each vendor. Creating a vendor inventory can highlight redundant vendors, vendors that are no longer used but that may still have access, and high-risk vendors.

Assess vendor risk. Each of your vendors will carry different levels of risk depending on the type of data they have access to, what they do with it, with whom they share it, and the kinds of controls they have in place to manage data. A vendor that's putting company logos on teddy bears for swag giveaways will carry less risk than a vendor that has access to customer data or your networks. You'll need to assess vendors' risk level before your company engages with them and on an ongoing basis afterward.

You can do this by creating a vendor risk assessment framework that classifies types of risk into tiers. This approach will help you focus your time, energy, and resources on higher risk vendors with more in-depth assessment and monitoring. It can also help reduce friction in selecting and onboarding new vendors. Tiers should take into consideration the type of information your organization shares with the vendor: whether it's confidential, personal, or if someone else having access would impact critical functions of your organization.

Vendor Risk Tiers

Tier 1

-A critical vendor where there's product dependency or where there is a significant business impact if there is an outage or failover.
-A vendor that is detailed in your DPA.
-A vendor that processes sensitive information, highly confidential information or employment-related data.

These vendors may require a PIA or other assessment. Examples include customer relationship managers, virtual servers, and more.

Tier 2

-A vendor you rely on to do your business but where there is less time-sensitivity associated with their offering.
-A vendor that processes confidential information or personal information (nonsensitive information).

An example might be a marketing agency that you use to support a campaign. While there might be time sensitivity with the marketing campaign, you might be able to send out materials the next day rather than right away (barring any time sensitivity related to crisis communications, of course).

Tier 3

-A vendor that processes less critical information.
-A vendor that helps you to achieve goals but with less business criticality.

An example might be an event planning service, SWAG creator, or design tool.

Another way to think of your risk tiers is by considering the total negative impact of a potential security or privacy event that could occur with a vendor, multiplied by the likelihood of that event occurring. If something is highly likely to occur but wouldn't have much of an impact, then that vendor would likely fall into a low-risk tier, and it's not worth the effort to mitigate that risk. On the other hand, if such an event with a vendor is unlikely to occur but would be totally catastrophic if it did, then it would be a high-risk tier, and it could be prudent to take some preventative measures.

Outside resources can help you assess vendor risk too. For example, Osano's vendor risk platform uses a vendor scoring system to help organizations see which vendors meet the highest privacy standards and which fall short at a glance. Something like this can help make vendor procurement repeatable and more consistent, and it can reduce time spent reviewing vendors. Another useful tool is SecurityScorecard, which measures vendors' cybersecurity risk and gives companies a sense of whether a vendor is reputable based on its score.

Select, onboard, and offboard vendors. Once a vendor passes your risk assessment and you decide to work with it, privacy has to remain paramount. Instances of selecting, onboarding, and offboarding vendors are critical moments because they involve either the sharing or careful retention of key data. You'll get your contracts in place during onboarding and familiarize your vendor with your privacy practices and your ongoing expectations. And offboarding is a critical time for handling and/or discarding data as relevant based on regulatory guidance.

Determine whether a data-protection impact assessment (DPIA) is in order. The GDPR requires a DPIA any time a data process uses new technologies or is likely to result in a high risk to the rights and freedoms of data subjects.[168] With this in mind, consider whether a DPIA is needed any time you engage a new vendor.

Continuously monitor vendor privacy posture. Vendor risk management is not a one-time activity. It's important to do your due diligence up front but then to keep up with it after the ink on the contract has dried. That means reviewing financial statements, evaluating SOC and other reports, and conducting internal audits of your vendors.

"Continuously" is the key word here. Even if a vendor checked all the boxes initially, it could introduce risk later. Every time something changes, a vendor needs to be reevaluated to ensure it's still in compliance and not introducing your company to undue risk. You can tether monitoring to your annual contract renewal with the vendor or to other benchmarks throughout the year. During monitoring, explore questions like: Are processing activities the same, or have they been adjusted? Do new DPIAs need to be performed? Is the vendor using AI? Are they handling data differently and/or in ways that do not align with your practices (i.e., sharing with new parties or making changes to their terms of service or privacy policy)? Have they been subject to legislation or suffered a data breach?

Regularly test your security measures. The GDPR requires data processors to regularly test, assess, and evaluate the effectiveness of their security measures for data processing.[169] Your vendor risk protocols play a huge role here, so make checking their efficacy a standard part of your workflow.

Secure your business continuity plan. We're about to jump into the specifics of developing your **incident response plan** in the event of a data-security incident. This is critical for knowing how you'll immediately respond to a data incident. It's also important to pan out to the larger picture. If a data-security problem requires you to change how you operate, what might that plan look like?

There's no doubt that vendor risk management is a big, ongoing job, but the more you automate, the less daunting it will be.

You can't ever set it and forget it—and you wouldn't want to. It's important to pay attention to what's going on with your vendors. But a robust vendor risk-management tool will streamline the moving parts and help your company stay as far away from vendor-related risk as possible.

. . . But Sometimes, Breaches Happen

A strong vendor risk management program will make your company risk resistant, but it can't ever be completely risk proof. Breaches can happen for reasons entirely out of your organization's control. And in those cases, *how you respond* can mean the difference between an event that devastates your business and a minor incident that actually reinforces your reputation as a trustworthy brand.

This is where your **incident response plan** comes in. If vendor risk management is a security system for keeping high-risk vendors away, your incident response plan is your strategy if a breach occurs despite your best efforts. You hope you'll never have to use it, but you need a plan in place so you can act immediately if needed. That plan includes knowing who on your team will do what and under which circumstances, what they'll say and to whom, and how your company will do its part to mitigate the incident's impact for all involved.

Your exact plan will depend on your organization's unique circumstances. Factors like the size of your security team, how often incidents occur, and the level of vendor risk you're exposed to will determine your approach. But, like vendor risk management, an incident response plan isn't just a nice-to-have. Data-privacy regulations such as the GDPR and CPRA require organizations to notify supervisory authorities and data subjects of breaches in certain circumstances. And your customers and employees expect you to do everything possible to keep their information secure—which includes having a plan to minimize damages when things go wrong. They likely won't check to see that you have an incident response plan just like they wouldn't ask whether your office building has fire extinguishers and a sprinkler system in the event of a fire. They just trust that those basic safety measures are in place.

A smart first step is to create an incident response team. This may be the same as your vendor risk accountability team. Your organization's data-protection officer, if you have one, would play a key role in incident response. Either way, be sure to have a team in place and train them to be fully familiar with your plan. This will minimize stress and build muscle memory for how to respond. Once your team is in place, these are the core elements to keep in mind as your organization creates an incident response plan:

Get familiar with breach notification and communication requirements. Work closely with your legal and privacy teams to ensure you understand your organization's obligations under data-privacy regulations. For example, the GDPR requires organizations to notify relevant supervisory authorities within seventy-two hours of becoming aware of a personal data breach if the breach puts data subjects' rights and freedoms at risk. That notification needs to include specific information, such as the nature of the breach and number of data subjects who were possibly affected; the likely consequences of the breach; and the measures your company had taken, or proposes to take, to address the breach and mitigate its adverse effects.[170] Similar requirements are in place for notifying data subjects depending on the circumstances. Most regulations also have requirements for documenting any personal data breaches so that supervisory authorities can confirm an organization's compliance with regulations. Usually, documentation needs to include the facts related to the breach, its effects, and the action your organization took to mediate the impact. Get familiar with what's required of you so you can act quickly to stay compliant and maintain trust with your data subjects.

Develop your notification and communication protocols.
Once you understand what's required of your organization
in the event of a breach, design protocols for decision-making, communication, and notification processes around those requirements.
Your vendor risk tiers will be helpful here. Consider creating processes
for how you'll respond in the event of a breach within each risk tier.
Have a plan in place for **what you'll say, who will say it,** and **to whom
you'll say it.** Remember that different circumstances will require
you to communicate specific messages to regulatory authorities, data
subjects, and/or other groups depending on regulatory guidance.

**Align your notification and communication protocols with your pri-
vacy practices.** This is one spot where a robust data-privacy program
shines. Depending on your data-handling practices and regulatory
obligations, you may not have to notify data subjects of a breach
if you've taken the appropriate measures to protect the personal
data affected by the breach. For example, Article 34 of the GDPR
says organizations are not required to communicate a data breach
to data subjects if they've implemented appropriate protection measures and those measures were applied to the personal data affected
by the breach. The article clarifies that the measures must render
the personal data unintelligible to any person who is not authorized
to access it, using methods such as encryption.[171] As you develop your
incident response protocols, make sure to sync them with your privacy
practices so each element operates as part of a unified system.

Make a plan to do what you say you'll do. Communicating the breach
as required is just one leg of your incident response plan. You need
to simultaneously do what your message promises you'll do to address
the breach. Remember that the GDPR requires organizations
to explain details including the nature of the breach, the likely consequences of the breach, and the measures your company will take
to mitigate its adverse effects. Other major regulations have similar

requirements. How you act on these items is up to you, but it usually includes three key actions:

- **Investigate.** Figure out what went wrong and then take action to ensure it will never happen again. To do this, you'll typically need to perform a forensic analysis of your IT systems to uncover where the breach occurred, what vulnerabilities were exploited, and whether malware or other malicious tools were involved.

- **Contain.** Create a plan for taking immediate action to contain a breach once it's confirmed. This usually involves isolating affected systems and patching up vulnerabilities to cut off further unauthorized access to data.

- **Mitigate.** Have a plan to help ease the impact of the breach for affected data subjects. This can include offering to fund tools such as identity theft protection or credit monitoring services. You'll also need to implement new security measures to avoid future breaches and potentially cut ties with any third parties associated with the breach.

Ultimately, a strong risk-management strategy is what makes a company resilient. The most trustworthy brands operate in the same ecosystem as those that succumb to data breaches and cyberattacks. They just have robust security measures in place that keep the bad guys out—and an incident response plan in place that zaps any problems that might come up, fast.

TL;DR CHEAT SHEET

- All companies are exposed to risk, and so is their consumers' data. Minimizing this risk and responding efficiently to any issues is what sets trusted brands apart.
- Any company is exposed to cybersecurity, legal, privacy, reputational, financial, and operational risks.
- You can be held accountable if a vendor or third party you share information with mishandles that data. Implement vendor risk management, or third-party risk management (TPRM), to minimize risks by vetting third-party privacy practices, spelling out privacy requirements in your contracts, and monitoring third-party practices over the term of the relationship.
- Make your company risk-resistant by setting up an accountability team; developing a control framework and risk methodology; utilizing a contracts management system; establishing processes for vendor vetting, onboarding, and monitoring; and using automation tools to streamline workflows.
- You can't avoid all risks, so you must have an incident response plan in place in case you suffer a data breach.
- Your incident response plan must include understanding and complying with your breach notification and communication requirements; effectively sharing your plan to investigate, contain, and mitigate a breach; and executing your plan.

Compliance Is Just the Beginning

I hope that after reading this book, you find the regulations and requirements surrounding data privacy much less daunting. Yes, it's a lot to take in, but you now know it doesn't need to suck up all your time, energy, and staff resources to become and stay privacy compliant. The good news is that you're now equipped to pivot and evolve as technologies develop, social perceptions evolve, and data privacy regulations continue to adapt. And all of those things *will* happen.

Plus, there's an upside to being the credible, solid, trustworthy Tom Hanks of privacy practices. Once you begin implementing what you've learned in this book, you'll likely experience a domino effect of benefits for your customers and your business. To start, being an exemplary data custodian inspires trust in your customers and makes you stand out from your competitors. But strong privacy practices can also give you data-driven insights that help you better serve your customers in ways you may have never realized they needed. Your customers' confidence in your company and your products and services are also likely to grow as a result of your transparency and privacy advocacy. This creates the competitive edge you need to enjoy sustainable growth.

Getting your data ducks in a row can also make parts of your job a lot easier. Operationalizing your program by focusing on the pillars set forth in this book (and using a privacy platform to streamline your processes) will help you collect, process, store, and manage data with agility as laws and industries evolve.

The time to get started is right now. We've entered a new era in which not actively causing damage is no longer good enough—not for inspired company leaders and not for our customers. We must lean into doing good and building successful companies while handling consumer data with the utmost respect and care. Whether we consider Google's old mantra of Don't Be Evil or the medical profession's creed of Do No Harm, when it comes to privacy practices, we all know better now, and therefore, we must do better.

It can be done by following the blueprint laid out for you in this book. Follow the steps, use Osano's free resources, and keep doing the good work that will set your company apart as a trustworthy brand.

ABOUT THE AUTHOR

Arlo Gilbert is the CEO and cofounder of Osano. An Austin, Texas, native, he has been building software companies for more than twenty-five years in categories including telecom, payments, procurement, and compliance.

In early 2018, Arlo and fellow cofounder Scott Hertel watched in disbelief as members of the US Congress questioned technology leaders about online data privacy. It was clear then, just as it's clear now, that even the best and brightest officials lacked essential knowledge about how data is stored and shared—and if they were confused, then businesses must be as well.

That's why Arlo and Scott founded Osano. Whether through his work as the CEO of Osano, as a thought leader on data privacy, or as a writer and speaker, Arlo has made it his mission to make it easy for businesses to do the right thing when it comes to data privacy.

ABOUT OSANO

Osano, the leading data-privacy management platform, empowers businesses to successfully navigate the complexities of privacy management by providing the necessary tools and insights for building, managing, and scaling holistic privacy programs. Designed with privacy professionals in mind, Osano's premier platform addresses the full spectrum of privacy needs, including assessments, vendor risk management, data mapping, and consent and subject rights management. As a public benefit corporation and certified B-Corp, Osano is dedicated to enhancing transparency and trust in the digital ecosystem. Emphasizing the critical role of privacy as a trust cornerstone, Osano upholds the belief that embracing privacy principles propels organizations into a place in the next wave of trusted brands.

ADDITIONAL RESOURCES

We have more resources, examples, and templates to help you build your privacy program than we can fit in this book. You can find them at osano.com/book. Some of the tools you can access there include:

- Privacy regulation cheat sheets and guides
- Sample data maps
- A RoPA checklist
- DPIA and PIA checklists
- Vendor assessment guides
- A comprehensive privacy policy checklist
- Examples of strong privacy policies
- A glossary of terms
- The privacy program maturity model

NOTES

1. Mike Schroepfer, "An Update on Our Plans to Restrict Data Access on Facebook," Meta, April 4, 2018, https://about.fb.com/news/2018/04/restricting-data-access/; James Sanders and Dan Patterson, "Facebook Data Privacy Scandal: A Cheat Sheet," *TechRepublic*, July 30, 2020, https://www.techrepublic.com/article/facebook-data-privacy-scandal-a-cheat-sheet/.

2. Matthew Rosenberg, Nicholas Confessore, and Carole Cadwalladr, "How Trump Consultants Exploited the Facebook Data of Millions," *New York Times*, March 17, 2018, https://www.nytimes.com/2018/03/17/us/politics/cambridge-analytica-trump-campaign.html.

3. "New Survey Finds Deep Consumer Anxiety Over Data Privacy and Security," Newsroom, IBM, April 16, 2018, https://newsroom.ibm.com/2018-04-15-New-Survey-Finds-Deep-Consumer-Anxiety-over-Data-Privacy-and-Security.

4. "Millions Choose Simple Privacy Protection with DuckDuckGo," DuckDuckGo News, DuckDuckGo, June 16, 2021, https://spreadprivacy.com/duckduckgrowing/.

5. Andy Yen, "There Are Now Over 100 Million Proton Accounts," Proton News, Proton, April 18, 2023, https://proton.me/blog/proton-100-million-accounts.

6. "Supplemental Info on Geofence Warrants in the United States," Services, Google, last modified August 17, 2021, https://services.google.com/fh/files/misc/supplemental_information_geofence_warrants_united_states.pdf.

7. "Apple Releases Report on Geofence Warrants and Data Requests," Apple, September 15, 2023, https://forums.appleinsider.com/discussion/233620/apple-releases-report-on-geofence-warrants-and-data-requests.

8. Sir Edward Coke, *The Selected Writings and Speeches of Sir Edward Coke, vol. I*, ed. Steve Sheppard (Indianapolis: Liberty Fund, 2003), https://oll.libertyfund.org/title/shepherd-selected-writings-of-sir-edward-coke-vol-i#lf0462-01_head_075.

9. "Parliament Passes the Quartering Act," History.com, November 13, 2009, https://www.history.com/this-day-in-history/parliament-passes-the-quartering-act.

10. *Eavesdropping*, Ian Potter Museum of Art, Liquid Architecture, and Melbourne Law School (2018), https://law.unimelb.edu.au/centres/iilah/news-and-events/2018-events-iilah/eavesdropping.

11. Thomas Jefferson et al, *The Declaration of Independence* (July 4, 1776), National Archives, https://www.archives.gov/founding-docs/declaration-transcript.

12. U.S. Const. amend. III § 2, https://constitution.congress.gov/browse/essay/amdt3-2/ALDE_00013335/.

13. "Yellow Journalism," PBS, 1999, https://www.pbs.org/crucible/journalism.html.

14. Samuel D. Warren and Louis D. Brandeis, "The Right to Privacy," *Harvard Law Review* 4, no. 5 (1890): 193–220, https://doi.org/10.2307/1321160.

15. William L. Prosser, Privacy, 48 CAL. L. REV. 383 (1960), quoted in Daniel J. Solove, *A Brief History of Information Privacy Law* in *Proskauer on Privacy* (Washington, DC: PLI, 2006), https://scholarship.law.gwu.edu/cgi/viewcontent.cgi?article=2076&context=faculty_publications.

16. Griswold v. State of Connecticut, 381 U.S. 479 (1965), https://www.loc.gov/item/usrep381479/.

17. "History of Data Protection," The Hessian Commissioner for Data Protection and Freedom of Information, accessed February 1, 2024, https://datenschutz.hessen.de/ueber-uns/geschichte-des-datenschutzes.

18. William Seltzer, "Population Statistics, the Holocaust, and the Nuremberg Trials," *Population and Development Review* 24, no. 3 (1998): 514, https://doi.org/10.2307/2808153.

19. Seltzer, "Population Statistics," 516.

20. Seltzer, "Population Statistics," 518.

21. Seltzer, "Population Statistics," 515.

22. Holocaust Encyclopedia, "Who Were the Victims," United States Holocaust Museum, last modified March 4, 2020, https://encyclopedia.ushmm.org/content/en/article/mosaic-of-victims-an-overview.

23. E. Fuller Torrey and Robert H. Yolken, "Psychiatric Genocide: Nazi Attempts to Eradicate Schizophrenia," *Schizophrenia Bulletin* (January 2010), https://www.ncbi.nlm.nih.gov/pmc/articles/PMC2800142/.

24. Torrey and Yolken; Robert N. Proctor, *Racial Hygiene: Medicine Under the Nazis* (Cambridge, MA: Harvard University Press, 1988): 189–191.

25. William Seltzer and Margo Anderson, "The Dark Side of Numbers: The Role of Population Data Systems in Human Rights Abuses," *Social Research* 68, no. 2 (2001): 484, http://www.jstor.org/stable/40971467.

26. Das Bundesarchiv, "Introduction: Ministry for State Security," accessed February 1, 2024, https://www.stasi-unterlagen-archiv.de/the-stasi/introduction/#c637.

27. Jan Freese, "The Swedish Data Act," *Current Sweden* (November 1977), The Swedish Institute, accessed in US Department of Justice, Office of Justice Programs Archive, https://www.ojp.gov/pdffiles1/Digitization/49670NCJRS.pdf.

28. Leah Collins, "Remember Foursquare? The Location Tech Used by Apple, Uber and Coca-Cola Knows You," June 16, 2022, CNBC Disruptor 50, CNBC.com, https://www.cnbc.com/2022/06/16/remember-foursquare-the-location-tech-used-by-apple-uber-knows-you.html.

29. "Data Broker Market: Global Industry Analysis and Forecast (2024-2030)," Maximize Market Research, accessed February 1, 2024, https://www.maximizemarketresearch.com/market-report/global-data-broker-market/55670/#details.

30. California Senate Bill No. 362, ch. 709 (2023), https://leginfo.legislature.ca.gov/faces/billTextClient.xhtml?bill_id=202320240SB362.

31. Kaveh Waddell, "Some Developers Don't Know What Their Apps Do with Your Data. Here's Why," *Consumer Reports*, March 13, 2020, https://www.consumerreports.org/electronics/privacy/developers-dont-know-what-their-apps-do-with-your-data-a1055672912/?utm_campaign=Newsletter&utm_medium=email&_hsmi=233290515&_hsenc=p2ANqtz--IwuKHYMSXsUZBR0aFkxfArZqjvxxQpj1TMscAnTa3P5AyEne947ZdM9m6xH-0ohAZ6F_PvdcpDaWRoN3oiB4DJRA0ww&utm_content=233290515&utm_source=hs_email.

32. "The Birth of the Web," CERN, accessed February 1, 2024, https://home.cern/science/computing/birth-web.

33. Mary E. Shacklett, "TCIP/IP," Tech Target Network, last modified July 2021, https://www.techtarget.com/searchnetworking/definition/TCP-IP.

34. Catherine Tan, "Does Log Data Count as Personal Data," Get Terms, The Privacy Hub, October 8, 2019, https://getterms.io/blog/does-log-data-count-as-personal-data.

35. Scott Crosby, "Urchin Software Corp.," Urchin Software Corp. Vault, September 2, 2016, https://urchin.biz/urchin-software-corp-89a1f5292999.

36. "Urchin Tracking Module," Google Support, accessed February 1, 2024, https://support.google.com/urchin/answer/28307?hl=en.

37. Randall Rothenberg, "An Advertising Power, but Just What Does DoubleClick Do?" *New York Times*, September 22, 1999, https://www.nytimes.com/1999/09/22/technology/an-advertising-power-but-just-what-does-doubleclick-do.html.

38. Rothenberg, "An Advertising Power."

39. Jeri Clausing, "U.S. Investigating DoubleClick Over Privacy Concerns," *New York Times*, February 16, 2000, https://www.nytimes.com/2000/02/17/\technology/us-investigating-doubleclick-over-privacy-concerns.html.

40. Joel Winston (FTC) to Christine Varney (representing DoubleClick), January 22, 2001, Legal Library, Federal Trade Commission, https://www.ftc.gov/legal-library/browse/cases-proceedings/closing-letters/doubleclick-inc.

41. New York State Attorney General, "Major Online Advertiser Agrees to Privacy Standards for Online Tracking," news release, August 26, 2022, https://ag.ny.gov/press-release/2002/major-online-advertiser-agrees-privacy-standards-online-tracking.

42. Thomas Baekdal, "The Original Cookie Specification from 1997 Was GDPR Compliant," *Baekdal/Basic Newsletter*, October 2019, https://www.baekdal.com/thoughts/the-original-cookie-specification-from-1997-was-gdpr-compliant/.

43. Shirin Ghaffary and Alex Kantrowitz, "Don't Be Evil Isn't a Normal Company Value. But Google Isn't a Normal Company," Vox.com, February 16, 2021, https://www.vox.com/recode/2021/2/16/22280502/google-dont-be-evil-land-of-the-giants-podcast.

44. Ghaffary and Kantrowitz, "Don't Be Evil."

45. Ghaffary and Kantrowitz, "Don't Be Evil."

46. Brian Clifton, "Google Analytics—Four Years On," *BrianClifton.com* (blog), April 16, 2009, https://brianclifton.com/blog/2009/04/16/google-analytics-fours-years-on/; Brian Clifton, *Advanced Web Metrics with Google Analytics*, 3rd Edition (California: Sybex, 2012), 18.

47. Brian Clifton, "Why Is Google Analytics Free," *BrianClifton.com* (blog), July 23, 2007, https://brianclifton.com/blog/2007/07/23/why-is-google-analytics-unique-free/.

48. "Web Analytics in AdWords," *Inside AdWords* (blog), Google, November 15, 2005, https://adwords.googleblog.com/2005/11/web-analytics-in-adwords.html.

49. Google 2006 Annual Report, United States Securities and Exchange Commission Archives, March 1, 2007, https://www.sec.gov/Archives/edgar/data/1288776/000119312507044494/d10k.htm.

50. Google 2009 Annual Report, United States Securities and Exchange Commission Archives, February 12, 2010, https://www.sec.gov/Archives/edgar/data/1288776/000119312510030774/d10k.htm.

51. Google 2008 Q1 Results, United States Securities and Exchange Commission Archives, April 17, 2008, https://www.sec.gov/Archives/edgar/data/1288776/000119312508083665/dex991.htm.

52. Seltzer and Anderson, "The Dark Side of Numbers," 484.

53. Human Rights Watch, "Break Their Lineage, Break Their Roots," news release, August 19, 2021, https://www.hrw.org/report/2021/04/19/break-their-lineage-break-their-roots/chinas-crimes-against-humanity-targeting#_ftn159.

54. Eryk Bagshaw, "Beijing's Video Game Crackdown Only Possible with No Privacy," *Sydney Morning Herald*, August 31, 2021, https://www.smh.com.au/world/asia/

beijing-s-video-game-crackdown-only-possible-with-no-privacy-20210831-p58nhs.html; Tom Singleton, "China Claims Youth Gaming Addiction Resolved," BBC.com, November 23, 2022, https://www.bbc.com/news/technology-63730316.

55. Anastasila Kruope, "Russia Uses Facial Recognition to Hunt Down Draft Evaders," Dispatches, Human Rights Watch, October 26, 2022, https://www.hrw.org/news/2022/10/26/russia-uses -facial-recognition-hunt-down-draft-evaders#:~:text=Moscow%20authorities%20are%20using%20 the,for%20Russia's%20war%20on%20Ukraine.

56. Ryan Phillips, "Infant Death Case Heading Back to Grand Jury," *Starkville Daily News*, May 8, 2019, https://www.starkvilledailynews.com/infant-death-case-heading-back-to-grand-jury/article _cf99bcb0-71cc-11e9-963a-eb5dc5052c92.html; Jia Tolentino, "We're Not Going Back to the Time Before Roe. We're Going Somewhere Worse," *New Yorker*, June 24, 2022, https://www .newyorker.com/magazine/2022/07/04/we-are-not-going-back-to-the-time-before-roe-we-are -going-somewhere-worse.

57. "Confronting Pregnancy Criminalization," Pregnancy Justice, Guide, July 2022, https://www .pregnancyjusticeus.org/wp-content/uploads/2023/09/1.Confronting-Pregnancy-Criminalization _6.22.23.pdf.

58. Kashmir Hill, "A Dad Took Photos of His Naked Toddler for the Doctor. Google Flagged Him as a Criminal," *New York Times*, August 21, 2022, https://www.nytimes.com/2022/08/21/technology/ google-surveillance-toddler-photo.html.

59. Kashmir Hill, "Her Child's Naked Dance Killed Her Google Account. New Appeals Path Restored It," *New York Times*, December 30, 2022, https://www.nytimes.com/2022/12/30/technology/ google-appeals-change.html.

60. Meg O'Connor, "Avondale Man Sues after Google Data Leads to Wrongful Arrest for Murder," *Phoenix New Times*, January 16, 2020, https://www.phoenixnewtimes.com/news/google-geofence -location-data-avondale-wrongful-arrest-molina-gaeta-11426374.

61. Nicole Valdes, "Valley Man Suing Avondale Police for False Arrest," ABC 15 Arizona, August 20, 2019, https://www.abc15.com/news/region-west-valley/avondale/valley-man-suing-avondale -police-for-false-arrest.

62. Jon Schuppe, "Google Tracked His Bike Ride Past a Burglarized Home. That Made Him a Suspect," NBC News, March 7, 2020, https://www.nbcnews.com/news/us-news/google-tracked- his-bike-ride-past-burglarized-home-made-him-n1151761.

63. Jim Mustian, "New Orleans Filmmaker Cleared in Cold-Case Murder; False Positive Highlights Limitations of Familial DNA Searching," Nola.com, March 12, 2015, https://www.nola.com/ new-orleans-filmmaker-cleared-in-cold-case-murder-false-positive-highlights-limitations-of- familial-dna/article_d58a3d17-c89b-543f-8365-a2619719f6f0.html; William Brangham, Nsikan Akpan, and Rhana Natour, "A Father Took an At-Home DNA Test. His Son Was Then Falsely Accused of Murder," *PBS News Hour*, November 7, 2019, https://www.pbs.org/newshour/ show/a-father-took-an-at-home-dna-test-his-son-was-falsely-accused-of-murder.

64. Ancestry.com, "Ancestry.com Launches New AncestryDNA Service: The Next Generation of DNA Science Poised to Enrich Family History Research," news release, May 3, 2012, https://www. ancestry.com/corporate/newsroom/press-releases/ancestrycom-launches-new-ancestrydna-service- next-generation-dna-science-0.

65. Mustian, "New Orleans Filmmaker Cleared."

66. Alfred Ng, "Police Say They Can Use Facial Recognition, Despite Bans," *The Markup*, January 28, 2021, https://themarkup.org/news/2021/01/28/police-say-they-can-use-facial-recognition -despite-bans.

67. Kashmir Hill, "Wrongfully Accused by an Algorithm," *New York Times*, June 24, 2020, https:// www.nytimes.com/2020/06/24/technology/facial-recognition-arrest.html; Steve Lohr, "Facial Recognition Is Accurate, if You're a White Guy," *New York Times*, February 9, 2018, https://www. nytimes.com/2018/02/09/technology/facial-recognition-race-artificial-intelligence.html.

68. Natasha Singer and Cade Metz, "Many Facial-Recognition Systems Are Biased, Says U.S. Study,"

New York Times, December 19, 2019, https://www.nytimes.com/2019/12/19/technology/facial
-recognition-bias.html.

69. John Simerman, "JPSO Used Facial Recognition Technology to Arrest a Man. The Tech Was Wrong," Nola.com, January 2, 2023, https://www.nola.com/news/crime_police/jpso-used-facial-recognition-to-arrest-a-man-it-was-wrong/article_0818361a-8886-11ed-8119-93b98ecccc8d.html.

70. Hill, "Wrongfully Accused."

71. Kashmir Hill, "Another Arrest, and Jailtime, Due to a Bad Facial Recognition Match," *New York Times*, December 29, 2020, https://www.nytimes.com/2020/12/29/technology/facial-recognition-misidentify-jail.html.

72. Jon Schluppe, "She Didn't Know Her Kidnapper. But He Was Using Google Maps—and that Cracked the Case," NBCNews.com, December 29, 2020, https://www.nbcnews.com/news/us-news/she-didn-t-know-her-kidnapper-he-was-using-google-n1252472.

73. FBI, "The FBI's Combined DNA Index System (CODIS) Hits Major Milestone," news release, May 21, 2021, https://www.fbi.gov/news/press-releases/the-fbis-combined-dna-index-system-codis-hits-major-milestone.

74. David Leins, "Tracked and Traced: Does Project Green Light in Detroit Reduce Crime?" Stories, Pulitzer Center, February 8, 2022, https://pulitzercenter.org/stories/tracked-and-traced-does-project-green-light-detroit-reduce-crime.

75. Grand View Research, *Location Intelligence Market Size and Trends*, Market Analysis Report, 2023, https://www.grandviewresearch.com/industry-analysis/location-intelligence-market.

76. "Supplemental Info on Geofence Warrants," Services, Google.

77. "Apple Transparency Report," Privacy, Apple.

78. Garance Burke and Jason Dearen, "Tech Tool Offers Police 'Mass Surveillance on a Budget,'" Associated Press, September 2, 2022, https://apnews.com/article/technology-police-government-surveillance-d395409ef5a8c6c3f6cdab5b1d0e27ef.

79. "How Google Uses Location Information," Google Privacy and Terms, accessed February 1, 2024, https://policies.google.com/technologies/location-data?hl=en-US.

80. Fernando Machado, "Burger King Fries Up 1 Cent Whopper Ploy," interview by Richard Quest, CNN Business, December 5, 2018, https://twitter.com/CNNBusiness/status/1070433884154691585.

81. David Griner, "After Trolling McDonald's, Burger King's App Was Downloaded 1 Million Times and Hit No. 1," *Adweek*, December 6, 2018, https://www.adweek.com/creativity/after-trolling-mcdonalds-burger-kings-app-was-downloaded-1-million-times-and-hit-no-1/.

82. Gabriel A. Fuentes, "In the Matter of the Search of: Information Stored at Premises Controlled by Google," Court Order, US District Court, ND Illinois, Eastern Division, August 24, 2020, https://static1.squarespace.com/static/5c1bfc7eee175995a4ceb638/t/5f4528d4ef2835252d794bfb/1598367957667/In+the+Matter+of+the+Search+of+Information+Stored+at+Premises+Controlled+by+Google.pdf.

83. Fuentes, "In the Matter of the Search of."

84. NY State Senate Bill S217, art.695 (2023), https://www.nysenate.gov/legislation/bills/2023/S217; https://legislation.nysenate.gov/pdf/bills/2023/S217.

85. Jen Fitzpatrick, "Protecting People's Privacy on Health Topics," *The Keyword* (blog), Google, May 12, 2023, https://blog.google/technology/safety-security/protecting-peoples-privacy-on-health-topics/.

86. Kashmir Hill, "Deleting Your Period Tracker Won't Protect You," *New York Times*, June 22, 2023, https://www.nytimes.com/2022/06/30/technology/period-tracker-privacy-abortion.html; Cynthia Conti-Cook, "Surveiling the Digital Abortion Diary," *University of Baltimore Law Review*, vol. 50, is. 1, art. 2 (October 28, 2020): https://papers.ssrn.com/sol3/papers.cfm?abstract_id=3666305.

87. Marlo McGriff, "Updates to Location History and New Controls Coming Soon to Maps,"

The Keyword (blog), Google, December 12, 2023, https://blog.google/products/maps/updates-to-location-history-and-new-controls-coming-soon-to-maps/.

88. Massachusetts Attorney General, "AG Reaches Settlement with Advertising Company Prohibiting 'Geofencing' around Massachusetts Healthcare Facilities," news release, April 4, 2017, https://www.mass.gov/news/ag-reaches-settlement-with-advertising-company-prohibiting-geofencing-around-massachusetts-healthcare-facilities; Assurance of Discontinuance Pursuant to G. L. 93A, § 5, Commonwealth of Massachusetts Superior Court, Digital Commons, https://digitalcommons.law.scu.edu/cgi/viewcontent.cgi?article=2452&context=historical.

89. Assurance of Discontinuance Pursuant to G. L. 93A, § 5, Commonwealth of Massachusetts Superior Court, Digital Commons, https://digitalcommons.law.scu.edu/cgi/viewcontent.cgi?article=2452&context=historical.

90. "Geofencing Market: Size Assessment and Trends (2023-2028)," Mordor Intelligence LLP, Report Linker, February 2024, https://www.reportlinker.com/p06483721/Active-Geofencing-Market-Size-Share-Analysis-Growth-Trends-Forecasts.html?utm_source=GNW.

91. Sam Biddle, "ICE Searched LexisNexis Database over 1 Million Times in Just Seven Months," *The Intercept*, June 9, 2022, https://theintercept.com/2022/06/09/ice-lexisnexis-mass-surveillances/; "Fighting Back Data Brokers," Just Futures Law, accessed February 1, 2024, https://www.justfutureslaw.org/fighting-data-brokers; "New Records Provide Details of ICE's Mass Use of LexisNexis Accurint to Surveil Immigrants," Just Futures Law Fact Sheet, June 8, 2022, https://static1.squarespace.com/static/62c3198c117dd661bd99eb3a/t/636028a3119908 67c6077887/1667246243453/Data-Brokers-Fact-Sheet-Final-6.8.22.pdf; Chris Mills Rodrigo, "LexisNexis under Growing Pressure to Sever Ties with ICE," *The Hill*, July 19, 2022, https://thehill.com/policy/technology/3564893-lexisnexis-under-growing-pressure-to-sever-ties-with-ice/.

92. Sam Biddle, "LexisNexis to Provide Giant Database of Personal Information to ICE," *The Intercept*, April 2, 2021, https://theintercept.com/2021/04/02/ice-database-surveillance-lexisnexis/; Award Profile Contract Summary, Definitive Contract PIID 70CMSD21C00000001, USASpending.gov, February 25, 2021, https://www.usaspending.gov/award/CONT_AWD_70CMSD21C00000001_7012_-NONE-_-NONE-.

93. Citaly Mora, "Activists Sue LexisNexis for Mass Collection and Sale of Personal Data of Millions," Illinois Coalition for Immigrant and Refugee Rights, August 16, 2022, https://www.icirr.org/News/Activists-Sue-LexisNexis-for-Mass-Collection-and-Sale-of-Personal-Data-of-Millions.

94. Mora, "Activists Sue LexisNexis."

95. Jesus Alvarado v. LexisNexis and Experian, US District Court, S.D. Cal., January 13, 2022, classaction.org/news/lexisnexis-experian-included-inaccurate-bankruptcy-info-in-consumer-reports-class-action-says#embedded-document.

96. Chris Riotta, "What Does the Federal Government Buy from Data Brokers," *NextGov/FCW*, August 17, 2022, https://fcw.com/congress/2022/08/what-does-federal-government-buy-data-brokers/375963/; Jane Edwards, "Reps. Jerrold Nadler, Bennie Thompson Inquire about Government Acquisition of Personal Data," ExecutiveGov.com, August 18, 2022, https://executivegov.com/2022/08/2-lawmakers-inquire-about-government-acquisition-of-citizens-personal-data/.

97. Fourth Amendment Is Not for Sale Act, S. 1265, 117th Cong. (2021), https://www.congress.gov/bill/117th-congress/senate-bill/1265/text.

98. Malia, "What Is the Difference Between Personally Identifiable Information (PII) and Personal Data," *TechGDPR* (blog), June 27, 2019, https://techgdpr.com/blog/difference-between-pii-and-personal-data/#:~:text=In%20a%20nutshell%2C%20PII%20refers,to%20an%20identifiable%2C%20living%20individual.

99. "Personally Identifiable Information," IAPP Resource Center, accessed February 1, 2024, https://iapp.org/resources/article/personally-identifiable-information/.

100. Harry Davies, "Ted Cruz Using Firm That Harvested Data on Millions of Unwitting Facebook Users," *Guardian*, December 11, 2015, https://www.theguardian.com/us-news/2015/dec/11/senator-ted-cruz-president-campaign-facebook-user-data.

101. Paul Grewal, "Suspending Cambridge Analytica and SCL Group from Facebook," Meta, March 16, 2018, https://about.fb.com/news/2018/03/suspending-cambridge-analytica/.

102. Grewal, "Suspending Cambridge Analytica."

103. Amy Held, "Facebook Says Cambridge Analytica Data Grab May Be Much Bigger than First Reported," NPR.org, April 4, 2018, https://www.npr.org/sections/thetwo-way/2018/04/04 /599542151/facebook-says-cambridge-analytica-data-grab-may-be-much-bigger-than-first-report.

104. Ashley Ahn, "Facebook Parent Meta Will Pay $7.25M to Settle a Privacy Suit over Cambridge Analytica," NPR.org, December 23, 2022, https://www.npr.org/2022/12/23/1145303268/ facebook-meta-cambridge-analytica-privacy-settlement.

105. Elizabeth Gibney, "The Scant Science Behind Cambridge Analytica's Controversial Marketing Techniques," Nature, March 29, 2018, https://www.nature.com/articles/d41586-018-03880-4.

106. Alexander Nix, "The Power of Big Data and Psychographics," Concordia Annual Summit, September 27, 2016, YouTube video, 3:40, https://www.youtube.com/watch?v=n8Dd5aVXLCc.

107. Nix, "The Power of Big Data," 3:15.

108. Nix, "The Power of Big Data," 4:04.

109. Nix, "The Power of Big Data," 4:15.

110. Nix, "The Power of Big Data," 5:40.

111. Nix, "The Power of Big Data," 8:00.

112. Stella U. Ogunwole, Megan A. Rabe, Andrew W. Roberts, and Zoe Caplan, "Population Under 18 Declined Last Decade," America Counts: Stories (blog), Census.gov, August 12, 2021, https://www. census.gov/library/stories/2021/08/united-states-adult-population-grew-faster-than-nations-total -population-from-2010-to-2020.html.

113. California Privacy Rights Act § 1798.155 (passed 2020), https://www.caprivacy.org/cpra-text/.

114. Venky Anant, Lisa Donchak, James Kaplan, and Henning Soller, "The Consumer-Data Opportunity and the Privacy Imperative," Our Insights (blog), McKinsey and Company, April 27, 2020, https://www.mckinsey.com/capabilities/risk-and-resilience/our-insights/the-consumer-data -opportunity-and-the-privacy-imperative.

115. "CCPA Out-Out Icon," State of California Department of Justice, accessed February 1, 2024, https://oag.ca.gov/privacy/ccpa/icons-download.

116. "94% of Consumers Want Control over the Information They Share with Companies," Venture Beat, June 24, 2022, https://venturebeat.com/data-infrastructure/report-94-of-consumers-want -control-over-the-information-they-share-with-companies/.

117. Sabra Ayres, "In the Online Austin ISD Mask Debate, a Strange Actor Emerges, Kazakhstan," Spectrum News 1: South Texas, El Paso, August 24, 2021, https://spectrumlocalnews.com/tx/south -texas-el-paso/news/2021/08/24/in-the-online-austin-isd-mask-debate--a-strange-actor-emerges --kazakhstan/.

118. Natasha Bertrand, "Russia Organized Two Sides of a Texas Protest and Organized 'Both Sides to Battle in the Streets,'" Business Insider, November 1, 2017, https://wcww.businessinsider. com/russia-trolls-senate-intelligence-committee-hearing-2017-11; Kevin Poulsen, Spencer Ackerman, and Ben Collins, "Russians Impersonated Real American Muslims to Stir Chaos on Facebook and Instagram," Daily Beast, September 27, 2017, https://www.thedailybeast.com/ exclusive-russians-impersonated-real-american-muslims-to-stir-chaos-on-facebook-and-instagram.

119. Sheera Frenkel and Daisuke Wakabayashi, "After Florida School Shooting, Russian 'Bot' Army Pounced," New York Times, February 19, 2018, https://www.nytimes.com/2018/02/19/technology/ russian-bots-school-shooting.html.

120. "Data Protection and Privacy Legislation Worldwide," UN Conference on Trade and Development, accessed February 1, 2024, https://unctad.org/page/data-protection-and-privacy-legislation-worldwide.

121. General Data Protection Regulation (2018), art. 5, https://gdpr-info.eu/art-5-gdpr/.

122. European Parliament, Council of the EU, Directive 2002/58/EC, "Directive on Privacy and Electronic Communications," July 12, 2002, https://eur-lex.europa.eu/legal-content/EN/ALL/?uri=CELEX%3A32002L0058.

123. "A European Strategy for Data," European Commission, February 19, 2020, https://eur-lex.europa.eu/legal-content/EN/TXT/PDF/?uri=CELEX%3A52020DC0066.

124. "A Guide to Lawful Basis," Information Commissioner's Office, accessed February 1, 2024, https://ico.org.uk/for-organisations/guide-to-data-protection/guide-to-the-general-data-protection-regulation-gdpr/lawful-basis-for-processing/.

125. "A Guide to Lawful Basis," ICO.

126. "When Can We Refuse to Comply with a Request," Information Commissioner's Office, accessed February 1, 2024, https://ico.org.uk/for-organisations/uk-gdpr-guidance-and-resources/individual-rights/right-of-access/when-can-we-refuse-to-comply-with-a-request/.

127. General Data Protection Regulation (2018), art. 27, https://gdpr-info.eu/art-27-gdpr/.

128. Jim Nash, "A Tri-Polar Privacy World: China, EU, US Conflict on Rights Regimes," *BiometricUpdate.com*, June 28, 2021, https://www.biometricupdate.com/202106/a-tri-polar-privacy-world-china-eu-us-conflict-on-rights-regimes.

129. Jaqueline Trevisan Pigatto, Mark W. Datysgeld, and Laura Gabrieli Pereira da Silva, "Internet Governance Is What Global Stakeholders Make of It: A Tripolar Approach," *Revista Brasileira De Política Internacional*, November 29, 2021, https://doi.org/10.1590/0034-7329202100211.

130. Nicholas Confessore, "The Unlikely Activists Who Took on Silicone Valley—and Won," *New York Times Magazine*, August 14, 2018, https://www.nytimes.com/2018/08/14/magazine/facebook-google-privacy-data.html?rref=collection%2Fsectioncollection%2Fmagazine&action=click&contentCollection=magazine&region=rank&module=package&version=highlights&contentPlacement=2&pgtype=sectionfront.

131. California Privacy Rights Act § 1798.140 (passed 2020), https://www.caprivacy.org/cpra-text/#1798.140.

132. Federal Trade Commission Act, 15 U.S.C. §§ 41–58 (passed 1914), https://www.ftc.gov/legal-library/browse/statutes/federal-trade-commission-act.

133. Richie Koch, ed., "What is the LGPD? Brazil's Version of the GDPR," GDPR.EU, accessed February 1, 2024, https://gdpr.eu/gdpr-vs-lgpd/.

134. Timothy Banks, "GDPR Matchup: Canada's Personal Information Protection and Electronic Documents Act," *Privacy Tracker* (blog), IAPP, May 2, 2017, https://iapp.org/news/a/matchup-canadas-pipeda-and-the-gdpr/.

135. California Attorney General, "Attorney General Bonta Seeks Information from California Employers on Compliance with California Consumer Privacy Act," news release, July 14, 2023, https://oag.ca.gov/news/press-releasesattorney-general-bonta-seeks-information-california-employers-compliance.

136. "GDPR Fines/Penalties," Intersoft Consulting, accessed February 1, 2024, https://gdpr-info.eu/issues/fines-penalties/.

137. "1.2 Billion Euro Fine for Facebook as a Result of EDPB Binding Decision," European Data Protection Board, May 22, 2023, https://edpb.europa.eu/news/news/2023/12-billion-euro-fine-facebook-result-edpb-binding-decision_en.

138. Identity Theft Resource Center, "Identity Theft Resource Center's 2022 Annual Data Breach Report Reveals Near Record Number of Compromises," news release, January 25, 2023, https://www.idtheftcenter.org/post/2022-annual-data-breach-report-reveals-near-record-number-compromises/.

139. "White Paper: The Osano Data Privacy and Data Breach Link," Osano, accessed February 1, 2024, https://www.osano.com/privacy-breach-link.

140. General Data Protection Regulation (2018), art. 13, https://gdpr-info.eu/art-13-gdpr/.

141. California Consumer Privacy Act § 11019.9 (passed 2018), https://leginfo.legislature.ca.gov/faces/codes_displayText.xhtml?division=3.&part=4.&lawCode=CIV&title=1.81.5.

142. General Data Protection Regulation (2018), art. 37, https://gdpr-info.eu/art-37-gdpr/.

143. California Privacy Rights Act § 1798.110 (passed 2020), https://www.caprivacy.org/cpra-text/.

144. General Data Protection Regulation (2018), art. 6, https://gdpr-info.eu/art-6-gdpr/.

145. California Consumer Privacy Act § 11019.9 (passed 2018), https://leginfo.legislature.ca.gov/faces/codes_displayText.xhtml?division=3.&part=4.&lawCode=CIV&title=1.81.5.

146. Kevin Litman-Navarro, "We Read 150 Privacy Policies. They Were an Incomprehensible Disaster," The Privacy Project, New York Times, June 12, 2019, https://www.nytimes.com/interactive/2019/06/12/opinion/facebook-google-privacy-policies.html.

147. General Data Protection Regulation (2018), art. 12, https://gdpr-info.eu/art-12-gdpr/.

148. IAPP, IAPP-EY Annual Privacy Governance Report, 2021, https://iapp.org/media/pdf/resource_center/IAPP_EY_Annual_Privacy_Governance_Report_2021.pdf.

149. General Data Protection Regulation (2018), art. 9, https://gdpr-info.eu/art-9-gdpr/.

150. "Data Protection Impact Assessments," Information Commissioner's Office, accessed February 1, 2024, https://ico.org.uk/for-organisations/uk-gdpr-guidance-and-resources/accountability-and-governance/guide-to-accountability-and-governance/accountability-and-governance/data-protection-impact-assessments/.

151. "When Is a DPIA Required," European Commission, accessed February 1, 2024, https://commission.europa.eu/law/law-topic/data-protection/reform/rules-business-and-organisations/obligations/when-data-protection-impact-assessment-dpia-required_en.

152. General Data Protection Regulation (2018), art. 25, https://gdpr-info.eu/art-25-gdpr/.

153. General Data Protection Regulation (2018), art. 5, https://gdpr-info.eu/art-5-gdpr/.

154. Federal Trade Commission, "Five Companies Settle FTC Allegations That They Falsely Claimed Participation in the EU-U.S. Privacy Shield," news release, September 3, 2019, https://www.ftc.gov/news-events/news/press-releases/2019/09/five-companies-settle-ftc-allegations-they-falsely-claimed-participation-eu-us-privacy-shield.

155. "Data Transparency's Essential Role in Building Customer Trust," Cisco, Consumer Privacy Survey, 2022, https://www.cisco.com/c/dam/en_us/about/doing_business/trust-center/docs/cisco-consumer-privacy-survey-2022.pdf.

156. General Data Protection Regulation (2018), art. 4, https://gdpr-info.eu/art-4-gdpr/.

157. California Privacy Rights Act § 1798.135 (passed 2020), https://www.caprivacy.org/cpra-text/#1798.135.

158. California Privacy Rights Act § 1798.100 (passed 2020), https://www.caprivacy.org/cpra-text/#1798.100.

159. "Austrian DPA Fines Postal Service over Data Disclosure Allegation; Italy's DPA Issues 3M Euro Fine," IAPP, October 21, 2021, https://iapp.org/news/a/austrian-dpa-fines-postal-service-over-data-disclosure-allegation-italys-dpa-issues-3m-euro-fine/.

160. "White Paper: The Osano Data Privacy and Data Breach Link," Osano, accessed February 1, 2024, https://www.osano.com/privacy-breach-link.

161. "Third Parties: Fast Growing Risk to an Organization's Sensitive Data," Help Net Security, November 20, 2018, accessed February 1, 2024, https://www.helpnetsecurity.com/2018/11/20/third-party-risks/.

162. Steve Alder, "Quest Diagnostics Facing Lawsuit for Disclosing Medical Information to Third Party Debt Collectors," HIPAA Journal, October 10, 2023, https://www.hipaajournal.com/quest-diagnostics-sued-patient-data-third-party-debt-collectors/#:~:text=Quest%20Diagnostics%20and%20its%20revenue,information%20exposed%20in%20the%20incident.

163. IBM, Cost of a Data Breach Report, 2023, https://www.ibm.com/reports/data-breach.

164. Joe Galvin, "60 Percent of Small Businesses Fold within 6 Months of a Cyber Attack. Here's How to Protect Yourself," Inc., May 7, 2018, https://www.inc.com/joe-galvin/60-percent-of-small-businesses-fold-within-6-months-of-a-cyber-attack-heres-how-to-protect-yourself.html.

165. "White Paper: The Osano Data Privacy and Data Breach Link," Osano, accessed February 1, 2024, https://www.osano.com/privacy-breach-link.

166. US Department of Justice, Criminal Division, Evaluation of Corporate Compliance Programs, Justice.gov, April 2019, https://www.justice.gov/criminal-fraud/page/file/937501/download.

167. Scott Julio, "21 Shadow IT Management Statistics You Need to Know," G2, October 28, 2020, https://track.g2.com/resources/shadow-it-statistics.

168. General Data Protection Regulation (2018), art. 35, https://gdpr-info.eu/art-35-gdpr/.

169. General Data Protection Regulation (2018), art. 32, https://gdpr-info.eu/art-32-gdpr/.

170. General Data Protection Regulation (2018), art. 33, https://gdpr-info.eu/art-33-gdpr/.

171. General Data Protection Regulation (2018), art. 34, https://gdpr-info.eu/art-34-gdpr/.

Made in United States
Troutdale, OR
01/03/2025

27565256R00163